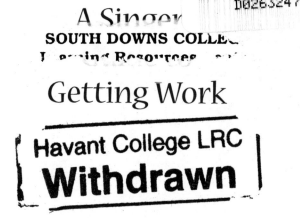

A Singer

Getting Work

A Singer's Guide to Getting Work

John Byrne and Julie Payne

A & C Black • London

First published 2003
A & C Black Publishers Limited
37 Soho Square, London W1D 3QZ
www.acblack.com

ISBN 0-7136-6424-X

A CIP catalogue record for this book is available from the British
Library.

A & C Black uses paper produced with elemental chlorine-free
pulp, harvested from managed sustainable forests.

Typeset in 10 on 12.5pt Sabon
Printed and bound in Great Britain by
Creative Print and Design (Wales), Ebbw Vale

Contents

Foreword

I never would have believed that anyone could put pen to paper and be able to sift out the pros, cons, ups and downs, ins and outs of a singer's life . . . but in this book John Byrne and Julie Payne have done just that.

One of my personal bugbears is the false sense of the entertainment industry that 'vote-for-a-popstar' type TV shows often give to up-and-coming hopefuls. They get splattered all over the front pages, get massive TV and Radio coverage and begin to believe they've made it . . . but success can often be short-lived, because there is NO 'quick and easy microwaveable cheesy' way to the top. There is only hard work and more hard work, practice and more practice. There is time put in at the expense of partying and having fun, and there might also be the added element of luck . . . cuz 'the harder you work, the luckier you get!'

For me, as a member of chart-topping The Three Degrees for over 20 years, this book conjured up memories of the not-so-glamorous early days when we had to design and sew our own costumes. (One time we even used a pair of gold brocade, satin-lined drapes that one of our mothers had in storage!) We paid our dues by rehearsing 8–12 hours a day to come up with original approaches to each new number, always looking for a new harmonic structure and how it would segue into the next song. Then after more hard work to choreograph the song, we had to fit it into our existing show in just the right place to pace it to a climactic ending.

We worked the 'club circuit' around the world, opening for the 'big guys' in Vegas, Miami, Atlantic City . . . and sometimes we died a death. After all, it wasn't us the audience had come to see. So we had to work all the harder to sell ourselves. We had to pick up our egos, rearrange our show and go back on again, learning all the time how the big stars like Sammy Davis, Nancy Wilson, Marvin Gaye, Tom Jones did it. Our idea was that if we ever got a hit record it would be the icing on the cake, because it was more important to learn how to *entertain* people so we could always work.

The club circuit is so much smaller today, especially in England, and it is almost impossible for newcomers to hone their skills as we did – but by reading this book you will get a valid, credible and honest take on how to approach getting work in today's musical climate.

Only perseverance will win out. Only dedication and focus will get you onto the first rung of the ladder. Only the ability to take criticism constructively will make you a better performer. And only a love for the art of singing will keep you in the business.

This book totally enthralled me. It conjured up so many memories of how I got to where I am today and, more importantly, how I stay there. Use it as your music 'how to' bible and you'll know you've done all the right things.

Sheila Ferguson

Dedications

JB: This book is for Candi Staton. Thanks for being obedient to what Jesus was doing through your life . . . and waking me up to what He was doing in mine.

JP: I'd like to dedicate this book to John for all the eternal motivation and repetitive kicks up my bum, his kind words and DRY jokes – I'd never known a real Angel 'til I met you; to family and friends for their encouragement and support, especially Herbie – love you, hope this book encourages you to execute your secret passion to sing!

Acknowledgements

Thanks to all the singers and aspiring singers we talked to and consulted for this text (whether or not your words made it into the book, they made it into our hearts!) To Brian Atwood, editor of *The Stage*, for allowing us to write the article that led to this book. To Bill Carpenter whose musical knowledge and enthusiasm and support for great singers continues to be an inspiration.

We are especially indebted to Dec Cluskey and Sheila Ferguson for making their time and vast experience available to us as they have done for so many others.

And one last dedication from both of us: to the unsung heroes and sheroes out there, yet to be discovered but who continue to inspire us on an hourly basis.

JB & JP

Introduction

So you want to be a singer?

Right at this minute we're not sure whether you want to sing blues like Bessie Smith, rock like Rod Stewart or even opera like Pavarotti – but we do know you've got one thing in common with all of those people: they had to start somewhere. We've written this book to get *your* career started as fast as we know how.

Of course, you may already be on the first steps of the singing career ladder.

If you're anything like us, you'll have discovered the ladder can be pretty shaky if you're relying on singing ability alone. Forging a successful career in any branch of performing arts involves a lot more than just performance – it also requires marketing and business skills, boundless confidence and positive energy, and most of all not just the ability to bounce back from the inevitable knockbacks and hiccups, but more importantly the ability to *learn* from them.

Collectively Julie and John have over 30 years' experience in show business, Julie as one of the top working singers in the country, John as a writer, performer and coach to actors, comics, presenters and producers, as well as singers. We both have a mutual interest in teaching as well as in performing, not to mention in talking nineteen to the dozen, which is how we started swapping ideas and experiences, and mentoring other singers (it's also why this book would have taken half the time to write if one of us had let the other get a word in edgeways!).

Over the years we've worked with singers at every level, from beginners to bona fide legends. One thing that's always fascinated us, though, is that despite the fact that most people we know have secret dreams of a singing career (including most actors, comics, presenters and producers), and there's now a whole industry of classes, tapes and TV shows offering to improve the singing bit, there's still precious little information generally available on the 'career' bit.

In this book we've tried to answer the questions beginners ask us most frequently, not to mention the questions we sometimes ask professionals whose careers aren't advancing as fast as they would like. You'll have noted that this book isn't called 'How to Become a Superstar Without Really Trying', because it's been our experience working with some very talented singers that when things go wrong it's not usually because they've invented some spectacular new mistake previously unknown in the history of music. It's usually because somewhere along the line they forgot something very basic, from looking after their voice, to looking after their fan base, to looking after the business side of their career.

In this book we've laid out as much of the basic information on building a singing career as we could remember. (Most of the important stuff was easy to remember, because we learned it through experiences we're going to try to help you *avoid*.) Since singing is such a diverse art we've also talked to a lot of fellow professionals about the things they wish they'd known when they were starting out.

But just as you can only learn to perform by actually performing, simply reading through these pages isn't going to help you build much of a career – you're going to have to try the tips and think through the questions raised for yourself .

It may be that some of the material here doesn't apply to your particular style or area of singing; it may be that some of the ideas don't suit your personality or your particular musical goals. But even finding out what doesn't work for you will bring you a step closer to discovering what does. (And if you do discover something new that works, don't forget to let us know in time for the second edition.)

Over the next hundred pages or so we'll be looking at everything from training your voice to performing effectively with it, creating your image to marketing it, all in the context of treating your showbusiness career like the business it actually is.

But every successful business needs a business plan, and every successful singer has a unique star quality all their own. We can help you with the planning bit, but the 'star quality' and 'uniqueness' is up to you.

Before you launch into the body of the book, take a few moments now to focus on your unique vision for your own career. Write it down, draw a picture, write a song about it – whatever helps you lock it into your sights. Maybe you're at the beginning of your singing journey and simply getting up on stage and doing a polished show is your goal. Maybe you've already been honing your skills on the amateur and talent show circuit and are toying with the idea of turning professional. Or maybe your vision involves your name in lights, world tours and making your own indelible mark on musical history. And why not? Some of music's biggest stars have come from the most difficult and unlikely beginnings.

Nor have you missed your shot if you didn't start making records at seven years old, despite what the current pop charts might have you believe. Your audience may be harder to reach, but if you really believe in yourself you'll put the extra effort into reaching them.

The clearer you make your vision, the easier you'll find it to judge which steps you need to take to make it a reality.

For now, we'd like to thank you for taking the step of reading this book for working singers. May it work in harmony with your singing talents to make all your career dreams come true.

Chapter One

Hitting the Right Note

Singing lessons for beginners . . . and professionals too

What are the basic requirements for being a working singer? Determination, certainly – a music career of any sort doesn't just happen overnight. Good organisational skills? Absolutely – at the beginning of your career you may well have to juggle your singing work with your 'day job' and at every stage of your performing career you'll find there's a lot more to keep track of than just performing. Do you actually need to be able to *sing*? Well, judging by some of the people already making a living from music – sometimes very high-profile people – we'd have to say that a good singing voice may not actually be essential, but hopefully most of our readers would agree that it certainly helps.

As with every other creative or physical talent, from drawing to playing football, an ongoing debate rages: does an individual have to be born with these gifts or can they be learned along the way? If we were to get fully into that debate it would take us all the way to the end of this book, and born talented or not, the reader would be left with as little chance of getting work as when they started, so we'll just point out that in our opinion most of us have a basic ability to do almost anything – but what determines success in any given field is not so much how *talented* we are, but how much *time and effort* we're prepared to put into developing that talent.

We know of amazingly gifted singers who never developed their ability, sometimes because they were too lazy but much more often because singing is just an enjoyable hobby, and they actually preferred to go to medical school, get married and have kids or study to become chartered accountants. (No, we can't understand that either.)

It's also fair to say that we know a number of professional performers who have voices ranging from average to 'couldn't hold a note with the help of superglue', but who by clever song selection, well-written patter or sheer unbridled belief in themselves have carved out successful and long-running careers.

If you're one of the latter performers, you may want to skip to later chapters of the book where we'll be looking at building a set which plays to your strengths and works with your weaknesses, but in all seriousness most people aspire to a singing career because they enjoy singing, and part of that enjoyment comes from developing your vocal abilities so that your voice does not just do what it can, but exactly what you want it to do.

That's where vocal training and practice come in, so with that in mind let's look at a few different types of voices, what they can do right now, and what vocal training could help them do better.

Different types of voices

The young beginner

With the girl/boy band phenomenon all the rage, and recent chart hits from pre-teen acts like S Club Juniors, it may seem that the average age of working singers is only now getting lower and lower, but in fact from the days of Shirley Temple and before, child performers have been a constant feature of the showbusiness scene.

In terms of vocal training, it's obvious that the earlier a singer starts taking care of their voice the better. But as far as vocal style is concerned, the voice, like every other aspect of a young person's make-up, continues growing and developing naturally throughout their lives.

Changes in voice are inevitable but the ability of 'grown up' child stars such as Aled Jones to sustain a career after their heyday can be directly related to good vocal habits learned early.

It also could be argued that the seeds of difficulty in the less happy careers of former child stars like Judy Garland or Frankie Lymon were also sown at an early stage.

In answer to parents who ask us what they should do with a child who shows singing ability our usual response is to find them a good singing teacher, give them lots of encouragement and then leave them to develop at their own pace.

The not-so-young beginner

Thankfully the education system is changing so that pupils are no longer forced to make a choice between creative subjects like art or music and only allowed do either if they're not good enough at engineering or science. The range of music taught in schools is also a lot wider, with everything from the Beatles to HipHop sharing the curriculum with more classical training or 'The Wheels on the Bus'.

But what about those of us who are way past school age and who didn't have the benefit of such enlightened education? Is it too late to think about rescuing our confidence and vocal abilities, never mind having the audacity to actually consider making singing a career?

Well, if we're over 18 it's unlikely we'll be auditioning for a boy or girl band anytime soon, but as we'll see later on in the book the charts are just the tip of the musical iceberg. There is work around for the older singer, but tapping into it is going to be down to the amount of time and effort we're prepared to put in now, both to developing our voice (which like other muscles may get a big shock if we haven't been developing it before) and to bringing whatever life experience we have had when we weren't singing into our vocal performances.

Remember that one of the essentials of a good performance is connecting with an audience, and most of our audiences will not be made up of professional singers but people with lives, and loves and dreams and disappointments just like us.

The self-taught singer

We could be wrong, but we doubt that many of the legendary blues singers from John Lee Hooker to Muddy Waters ever had singing lessons in their lives. So we certainly have no grounds for arguing that vocal training is essential for musical success. However, the blues is a musical *tradition* passed down from person to person, and even the great blues performers developed their style by listening to and watching older performers, borrowing vocal techniques and adding them to their own style.

Many self-taught singers have developed very individual styles and fear that vocal training will somehow stifle their natural abilities and turn them into something they are not. Assuming the singing teacher is a good one, that shouldn't happen – in fact the focus will be on developing whatever vocal ability is already there, and most importantly correcting any bad habits which may have crept in so that the voice not only sounds better but is looked after properly.

The Who may have sung about hoping they died before they got old, but there are quite a few self-taught rock singers who have made it alive into middle age – unfortunately some of them have done serious damage to their vocal chords along the way.

The professional and classically trained singer

Surely someone who's making a living as a singer already doesn't need training? Well in any business it's not usually enough to keep up with the game. In order to really prosper you've got to keep *ahead* of the game, and singing is no different. It's obvious that styles of singing change pretty quickly – in the 1950s almost every male rock singer aped Elvis Presley's 'uh-huh-huh' vocal style, but such an approach would sound pretty dated today (unless it's an Elvis remix, of course). On the other hand contemporary stars like Robbie Williams have broadened their appeal by dipping back into the Swing era and adopting a crooning style with its very distinctive laid-back mannerisms.

It's not unknown for classical singers to try a little jazz or rock singing to achieve more looseness or expressiveness, while when Julie worked with Soul II Soul she was dispatched to an opera teacher to brush up on her vocal clarity.

As with any other instrument, the more versatile you can be with your voice the more opportunities you'll have for making a living from it, and a little extra tuition now and then is not so much an expense as a career investment.

Finding your teacher

For the moment let's assume that you're not signed up to a top label or management company, so the chances of having David and Carrie Grant flown down to your mansion for private lessons are pretty slim, and you may not have all that much cash to invest. So how do you find some decent singing tuition, and when you've found it how do you make the best of it?

At the beginning of the book we noted that carving out a singing career can involve using your voice in as many different ways as possible, and one way many working singers fund their own careers is by giving singing lessons to others.

The result is that finding someone offering singing lessons in your local area shouldn't be too difficult at all – a quick look at the small ads in your local paper, the noticeboard of the corner shop or an enquiry in the local library should throw up quite a few possibilities. Working out which teacher will give you best value for your hard-earned cash is another job entirely.

A good first step is to phone up several teachers, tell them briefly what your goals are, and see what their response is and how much they charge. If nothing else this will give you a good idea of what the going rate is for singing lessons in your area.

Most singing lessons last for three-quarters of an hour to an hour, although it may be possible to book a double session. It is usual for the student to travel to the teacher, who often works at home or in a hired room. If you're an absolute beginner to singing (and even if you're not) a good plan is to try to negotiate a free sample lesson to see if the teacher's style suits you and if you suit the teacher. Many established singing teachers offer this already, and if they do it's usually a good sign that they have confidence in their abilities.

Your first impressions of the proposed teacher are very important – as a beginner you may not be in a good position to judge how proficient the teacher is, but you'll at least get a feel for whether you feel comfortable with them or not. Since no teacher no matter how good can work miracles in just one session, it's important to find someone you feel comfortable with – after all, you're liable to be spending a lot of time in their company.

Professional qualifications, whether in music or teaching music, are obviously one good indicator that a tutor knows what they are talking about, although it must be said that just because someone is gifted themselves in a particular area, doesn't *necessarily* mean they have a gift for teaching it to others.

Feel free to ask questions about the teacher's own career and training. Most will be very happy to volunteer the information, and it can certainly be an advantage to be taught by someone who is actively working as a musician themselves.

On the other hand, older professionals who have retired from performing can have a wealth of experience to share, and if their technique is solid, can still have a lot to teach even the youngest and most contemporary students.

Whatever the age or background of your prospective teacher, make sure they genuinely understand and are enthusiastic about your own singing goals. If you want to sing rock and your teacher is operatically trained it can be as much an advantage as a disadvantage . . . but if your tutor turns up their nose at the drop of a power chord it's not going to be a very happy relationship for either of you.

Bear in mind also that while it's useful to know about your tutor's career background the focus of each singing lesson should be on *you*, not on a running commentary of their own day-to-day adventures and misadventures in the music business or other aspects of their personal lives. You are paying the money and you are entitled to get your money's worth.

Having said that, all your tutor can do is guide you in developing your vocal skills – the practice is very much up to you. There's a saying that of all musical training, singing lessons are the least valued and have the highest drop-out rate. The reason is pretty clear when you think about it – almost any other music lesson involves the purchase of an instrument, and just like membership of a gym, it's the spending of money which often acts as a motivation to continue classes despite whatever other distractions get in the way.

With vocal training you were already given your 'instrument' for free, so how much you put into your voice lessons very much depends on how much you value the gift you've been given.

Continuing the gym analogy, there is an ongoing debate among athletes about how many workout sessions per week lead to optimum fitness, and a really keen singing student may also wonder if more singing lessons will mean more and faster progress. Our experience is that at the beginning, one lesson a week is enough as long as you are prepared to practise the things you've learned every other day of the week.

As with any other physical activity one of the goals of singing tuition is to build good habits, and it's repetition that achieves this. Short, regular practice periods each day will achieve a lot more than cramming the night before the weekly lesson.

Many tutors offer (and if they don't, it may be possible to negotiate) a discount 'block' of lessons – for instance if you book four weekly lessons in advance you get an extra one free. Besides saving you money if you can afford an upfront payment, parting with the cash in advance is increased motivation to turn up to the lessons and put in the practice needed.

Every singing teacher will have their own way of working, but the basic lesson should include some work on breathing and relaxation, practice with scales and vocal delivery . . . oh, and it's usually a good idea if you get to sing a song or two.

How these elements are balanced will depend on a mixture of the teacher's approach and your own taste, but even if the bulk of the lesson revolves around going over techniques, it makes sense to put them into practice on some proper songs at the end – after all, a paying audience isn't going to want to hear you practising your scales. On the other hand, once you've learnt to open your mouth and make a sound which is roughly in tune, and can breathe in approximately the right places (and for some of us, this can take some time), it's good to have a tutor who keeps stretching us, and encouraging us to do a little better than we thought we could do.

The nature of one-to-one singing lessons is that a friendly and familiar atmosphere can develop between tutor and student, and this is no bad thing, but if your lessons are turning into an uncritical mutual 'chat and karaoke' session, maybe you'd be better off saving your money for spending down the pub.

Most singing teachers can play piano or another instrument, if not to concert standard then at least enough to demonstrate scales or accompany you on simple tunes. Some will encourage you to bring along CDs with backing tracks to songs you want to sing. This is not to say that you should feel cheated if your tutor works on vocals only, but if the style of music you would like to sing isn't unaccompanied folk madrigals it's usually a good idea to get in the habit of singing to music early on.

One way to keep a check on both you and your tutor is to tape yourself as your lessons progress (again, a good tutor will encourage this). As you listen to the tapes from month to month you should notice continuous improvement; if not – and assuming you are keeping your practice up – it may be time to find a new approach or perhaps a new teacher.

As with any other service, you are entitled to expect good professional conduct from your singing tutor whether they operate out of their bedsit or an office in music college. Equally, try to get in the habit of taking your lessons seriously yourself. Turning up on time, for instance – quite often tutors timetable several lessons with different people back to back, and if you turn up late there may be no flexibility at the other end to extend your lesson. On the other hand if the student before you has turned up late – even if they are a West End star – you are perfectly within your rights to expect to start your own lesson on time. Singing tutors, like any other teacher, should not 'play favourites'.

Lest all of the above should sound cynical and gloomy, it's worth stating that the majority of singing teachers are very professional and committed, and quite a few singers who are perfectly capable of earning a decent living entirely from their own vocals continue teaching purely because they enjoy encouraging others to develop their musical gifts. If the first few tutors you come across don't seem quite right, keep looking – the singing tutor you can work with can become a vital part of your 'support team'.

Many singers even when they have completed their basic training will book in for refresher lessons with a favourite tutor every so often just to keep on top of their game, and a special lesson before a big audition can be money very well spent.

Formal education and full-time courses

If you have the time and money, you may want to pursue a formal music education. There are many different types of courses and colleges available both full time and part time, so step number one is simply to get hold of as many brochures and prospectuses as you can and see what's on offer. In some cases courses focus on music only, while theatre schools tend to concentrate on a variety of skills such as drama and dance along with singing. Certainly any extra skills you learn can only help your career, but if your focus really is on singing many of the courses (which quite often include a lot of theory as well as practical work) may be too academic or broad-based for you.

You will also find that a lot of the courses involve an audition as part of the application. We will be looking at general auditions later on in the book (chapter four), and many of the points you will find in that section apply to auditions for courses, too. It's true also that there is a lot of competition to get on most of the best-regarded courses. But if you are nervous about the auditions or interviews it's worth remembering that in considering people for courses, the panel are not necessarily looking for the *best* singers, they are looking for the most *promising* singers – the ones who will benefit most from what's being offered on that particular course of study.

If you feel you lack experience, well, you wouldn't be applying for a course if you had the experience already, would you? And your commitment, enthusiasm and clearly thought-out goals may be just as much a factor in the final decision as the quality of your voice.

On the other hand, if you do get turned down for a particular course it doesn't automatically mean that you are 'aren't good enough', it can simply be that the panel has decided that with your particular level of ability or interests you would not get the full benefit from this particular course.

Trust us: with the amount of time, energy and money you'll need to invest in full-time or even part-time music study, being stuck on a course that doesn't appeal to you can be a huge source of grief for all concerned. Chalk it up to experience (you'll find yourself doing a lot of that as your career progresses) and turn your efforts back to finding a course that does suit you.

It goes without saying that formal education of any sort, especially for adults, tends to be expensive. Unfortunately singing isn't high on the list of funding priorities for most organisations, but it is certainly worth checking with your proposed college or other information sources to see if there are sponsorships or trust funds available.

Of course, you don't have to wait till you graduate to put the job-finding skills that come later in this book to good use – the need to fund your studies can be a very good motivation to start trying to make money from your singing as soon as you possibly can!

Adult education and part-time classes

The growing interest in singing as a career means that many adult education and youth centres run evening and weekend classes and courses ranging from 'singing for the tone deaf' through masterclasses in jazz, opera and world music to 'the power of the healing voice'. In general you don't have to audition to get into these kinds of classes – in fact the only qualification is the ability to turn up on enrolment evening and pay the fee. But they are often taken by very expert and committed teachers and can be a very good way of practising your singing in the company of others.

In most cases, the class set-up means there will be a lot of communal singing as well as one-to-one tuition, and with this in mind it's important to remember that most people sign up to have a good time first, and to learn second. If you're hyper-focused on your career you may find the general ribbing, giggling and flirting a bit off-putting . . . mind you, you won't find things so different backstage at some professional gigs so you may well have to get used to it.

And speaking of professional gigs, one of the principal motivators for any kind of training, especially in the early stages, is to focus on your vision and goals – the place where all this practising and hard work will lead.

Your career as a singer can take you in quite a few different directions, so before we start to map out the different parts of the journey, let's use our next chapter to identify your individual destination. After all, knowing where you want to go is probably one of the most useful factors in selecting the right teacher or coach to be your guide.

Chapter Two

Do You Know Where You're Going To?

Exploring your career options

Leaping from our first chapter on singing lessons right into the jobs market may seem like putting the cart before the horse. But as we have already said, on any journey you can't work out a route until you know where you're going, so with this in mind, this chapter is a quick overview of the different areas where you can expect to ply your vocal trade.

As with people in any other creative field, each singer has their own strengths and weakness, likes and dislikes, and finding the niche which best suits you as a person and a performer can be a giant step towards making that particular area your own.

Probably most of us who start out as singers are initially influenced in our career choices by the singers we admire ourselves. In fact if we could be them and have their careers we'd be entirely happy. Of course, most of our heroes have put a lot of hard work into being themselves and building those careers, and that's what lies ahead of us too, which is all to the good because as we start to develop our own careers we also start to develop our own unique style – and perhaps even discover some areas of the music business we hadn't considered before. George Strait, probably the model for all of the modern country singers, started off in a rock band, while Philadelphia Soul legend Sheila Ferguson's original role model was entertainer Nancy Wilson.

In order to increase *your* chances of becoming a role model to the next generation of singers, let's start off this overview of singing careers by looking beyond the obvious horizon where most musical ambitions stop and start.

Making the charts

No matter how many 24-hour cable and satellite channels
spring up devoted exclusively to music, no matter how many
new technological innovations emerge with music marketing on
the Internet, there seems to be one big emotional goal for every
British performer: the first appearance on *Top of the Pops*. No
matter how street cred or 'alternative' musicians affect to be,
most of them have admitted that it was being seen on the
nation's number one chart show that convinced their mates and
their mums that they were actually getting somewhere in the
music business.

At the time of writing the charts are overrun with
manufactured boy and girl bands with an average age of 16,
and the general perception is that the record industry is so
commercialised and cut-throat that getting anywhere without a
powerful label behind you and blanket promotion in the
megastores is a huge mountain to climb. But it's still a fact that
for most singers the most visible representation of career success
is appearing in the pop charts or on TV music shows.

So is breaking into the charts as hard as everyone says it is?
Yes. Is it impossible? No.

No matter how streamlined and manufactured the music
industry becomes, independent music still does make it into the
charts: older singers like Gordon Haskill can still have number
one hits, and in the case of Eva Cassidy or Elvis, deceased
singers and styles of music which appear to have had their day
can make a comeback if they catch the public imagination.

Remakes of popular classics tend to do well, probably
because they appeal to two main audiences: the current, record-
buying young people hearing the tune for the first time, and the
older fan who has fond memories of the tune and is suitably
impressed by the reworking of it.

Equally, the record industry can pour huge amounts of
money and energy into acts and recordings which either never
make it or, like TV band Hear'Say, fall apart under too much
exposure.

It's also true that there are very few artists like Madonna or
Elton John who have managed to sustain chart success over a
long period of time – for most artists one or two chart hits are
the basis on which they build a touring career and direct sales

to their own fan base – in many cases several decades after they had their own chart success.

Former chart stars like Cathy Dennis have used their own pop-star experiences to fuel much more successful and long-term careers writing and producing for the chart acts of today, but in the main, chart success can be fleeting even for acts that do make it. If chart success is your driving goal, it's best to make it part of your overall career plan rather than your ultimate goal.

The average lifespan of a chart act used to be about two years; these days it can be as little as two weeks. So whilst you seek your chart goals it's always a good idea to get to grips with other aspects of the record business, such as songwriting, producing, engineering, even management. That way you could enjoy a different kind of chart success and longevity

Despite the picture the celebrity magazines present, if hitting the charts is part of your agenda you'll need to take the whole business very seriously. On the other hand, if you see yourself as a 'serious' singer you will need to lose any 'snobbishness' you may have about chart music despite what you may think about the musical quality of current hit records.

Dec Cluskey, lead singer of the Bachelors, one of the most successful chart groups of the 1960s and '70s (they outsold the Beatles) and still at the forefront of today's music scene as a mentor to up-and-coming artists, knows more than most about music and production, and has no time for 'musos' who whinge and moan about the 'quality' of the charts. You'll be hearing more from Dec later in the book (and maybe even have the chance for him to mentor you), but for now take on board Dec's advice that the majority of people who moan about the quality of the pop charts *never had* any chart hits. Whether or not the music in the charts is to your taste is immaterial. Listen without prejudice to any chart record and it is likely to have top quality production and excellent vocal arrangements – you need to aim for the same excellence in every aspect of your work. And if you do want to get into the charts, you need to sound like what is in the charts right now, not what you personally would like the charts to sound like, or what the charts used to sound like when you were buying singles. Even the 'wild cards' like Gordon Haskill or Eva Cassidy conform to the standards of top production values and good vocals.

If you haven't watched *Top of the Pops* or other chart shows since the Boomtown Rats were number one it's time to do some serious research. It's hard to write a novel if you don't read novels, it's hard to write a play if you don't go to plays, and – regardless of how much you know about music in general or how much stage experience you have, it's next to impossible to have a chart hit if you don't know what's in the charts right now. Start watching and listening to every chart show around, and watch with your brain switched to analytical. What is it about the lyrics, the bass line, the vocal performance, the look that makes a particular act or song 'chartworthy?' Once you've identified common factors in the current chart songs, start listening to up-and-coming performers and tracks and see if you can identify the releases which will be hits *next month*. If you're not a teenager start talking to teenagers and find out what kind of music they are buying or listening to. If you *are* a teenager pay particular attention to the chart songs you *don't* personally like. Is there an element you can add to your own style to create a new angle on something that already works? Most of all, immerse yourself in the music press, and no we don't mean *Smash Hits* or even *NME*. (Check the resource section at the end of this book for music trade papers.) Get to know not just the latest music fashions but more importantly the people behind them, and that means record executives and A & R (artists and repertoire) people as much as hot producers. These are the 'gatekeepers' you need to get your work in front of (we'll be looking at marketing yourself in detail later on), and you need to know their likes, dislikes, aims and interests.

And after all that, will you get a chance at chart success? Well, maybe. And please, if you do make it to Top of the Pops, email us (webtoonist@eircom.net) so we can sit with our mums and mates and watch you.

The good news, though, is that even if you never make it to number one or even number 100, and especially if chart success isn't even your interest, this most visible form of music career is just the tip of the iceberg. Take a look through *The Stage* and other theatre papers and you'll find there are hundreds of vocalists, none of whom are household names (although many are very respected within the industry), making a living as working singers. In the pages that follow we'll take a closer look at what some of them are up to and how you might take a leaf out of their book. For starters, here are quotes from three hardworking singers currently making a living in two very different music arenas.

Enyonam Gbesemete

'I've been in this business about 15 years doing studio sessions and working with various bands. I've done the gig circuit of clubs, pubs, restaurants, etc. as well as loads of private events, weddings, etc. I am now singing in theatre and my advice to anyone following along those lines is get some form of training. You'll need the stamina. I didn't start off wanting to sing in theatre and so was not prepared physically or vocally for eight shows a week. Investigate. Everything for me happened by chance and I'm still learning as I go along. You need to have your head screwed on. I'm the type of person as long as I'm *in* the business doing what I'm doing I'm happy. Even though I'm in the ensemble I'm a vital part of the show and you have to feel that way otherwise there's no point in doing it. I'm very self-confident and have lots of belief in myself, which is good. You also need to be as versatile as possible so that you can go up for more jobs. But there comes a time when you have to start turning down certain jobs in order to secure better ones. The favours have to stop and you need to start getting paid for everything you do. If you're renowned for just one role people will only ever offer you that type of role, and if they know you'll do it for little or no money that's how they'll treat you. It is hard. Like any other job there's a ladder you have to climb.

Initially, I didn't miss the live circuit gigs and theatre was something exciting which I hadn't done before. Gigging is a series of short contracts and you get to travel around a lot and work for lots of different people. But theatre is more steady and the contracts can be longer, giving you a sense of security.'

Roy Hamilton

'I've been doing this for about 20 years. Back in the early days there were a lot more big tours around which were better paid. Going back about 10 years there were more live bands and less performing to minidiscs. I sing soul, jazz, R & B, old school stuff like Lonnie Liston Smith, Roy Ayres, James Brown and, dare I say, Barry White! These classic artists have produced some classic hits and these appeal to all age groups. I usually work with people that are great musicians because there's less chance of you doing a bad gig! Try to be selective. Don't accept every single job. I tend to work with established people who I either know or who have been highly recommended. I think it's very important to be out there knowing who's who. As a singer you have to know the best keyboard players, the best guitarists, etc. so that when you get together as a band you've got the cream of the crop who are all on the case. Singing is my only source of income and I've earned most of my keep doing studio sessions and live gigs. Mind you, I almost went on tour with the musical *Hair*. I got through all the auditions and had even started rehearsals. But I also had a recently released song that had entered the charts, and was advised by the record company that I'd need to be available to do promotional stuff. And might be over-exposed in the wrong arena. My simple advice would be to network, Get out there and get yourself known. Beware of clique circles. When people have to dep. out a gig [i.e. ask someone else to take it over] they usually do it within their little circle of friends and acquaintances. If you're only familiar with one circle you deny yourself the full scope of opportunities. A lot of my work comes via word of mouth. If I do a bad job it'll be on the head of the person who put me forward for the gig. And vice versa. It's hard work sometimes, especially when gigs are scarce, but there are loads of great opportunities to do the thing you love best and get paid for it!'

Mary Pearce

'I've been in showbiz 12 years. The most terrifying gig was probably Glastonbury, performing to 8,000 people. The sun was beating down and although my top half was in the shade, the sun was burning my feet. I remember getting real bohemian and taking my shoes off. I was also having a bad hair day but had forgotten my wrap for my hair so I ended up having to unpick the plaits with my fingers into a big afro! I was on tour with nine men. I was the only woman – it was wonderful and I was treated like a precious stone. If there were only two dressing rooms I would always get one of them. I'm not one of those women who needs her bags carried, but if there was a situation where one of the guys had to lift it for me they didn't mind. As for me, I believe that if you packed it you carry it! Learn to pack your bag effectively. The sort of things you should pack, a contingency-planned outfit – sometimes you can get delayed and might not have time to change, so don't dress like a tramp for the journey. I love being the only woman on the tour. I didn't become a lad – on the contrary I made the lads become girls, I got them shopping for domestic stuff and cosmetics and soon enough they were asking me for manicures! They became very conscious of their personal appearance, their wardrobes, etc.

I spent three years doing lead vocals for Courtney Pine, who was already an established jazz musician when I joined the band. We went all over the world. Courtney always used to say 'My gigs are the same, but different – no two gigs are the same. That's what makes it exciting.'

I got by quite well without an agent but now belong to an agency called Hobsons who get me a lot of advertising work, e.g. with Specsavers – I sang the vocal for the TV ad. However, most of my work is by word of mouth. As much as 80 per cent. It's important to be nice but more important to be professional. You can be as nice as you want but if you're late and your voice is tired you'll be remembered for being the nice vocalist with the tired voice who comes late! Oh, by the way – make sure you smell nice. You have to spend a lot of hours in confined spaces – the actual recording area of some studios is really tiny. If you have BO or bad breath it can be unpleasant for those around you, and vice versa. Sounds bitchy I know – I've probably got a bit of a reputation for being a bit of a bitch but most of the time that's just me being professional, not skylarking, and getting on with the job in hand.

I haven't done duet gigs for a long time. But when I did, I was probably quite spoilt at being able to always book a competent musician. You make sure that you learn all the correct words so that if you have to work with a musician who doesn't know you and how you work and all your hand signals then at least you can't be faulted if he makes a mistake. You may find that you have to direct the musician by calling the bridge, chorus, verse, solo, etc.

I was a signed recording artist. That was probably the hardest work – dance music, working with a band called Up Your Ronson for about three years. At first it meant doing a lot of PAs (personal appearances), sometimes more than one on the same night. I once did three as far afield as Sheffield, Burnley and London in one night. You learn that you cannot be drinking alcohol at all until the gig is over – only then can you relax. You have to be on point at all times. Get loads of sleep and *no smoking on the tour bus – pleeeeeezzzzz!* Speaking of the 'tour bus': what happens on the bus stays on the bus and that is my final word on that one – I have too many friends to lose!'

Live vocalists

Yes, beyond MTV and the box, away from the racks of Tower Records and HMV, ignored by the celebrity gossip columns there is a whole army of singers young and old like Roy, Enyonam and Mary carving out a living from singing live. An even greater number of singers are still working in day jobs, but get to spend their evenings doing something they love and making a little extra money in the process. And if their profile seems a little less glamorous than the next big pop idol, remember that the next big pop idol is probably out there somewhere too, learning the ropes of performing live and entertaining an audience before that 'big break'.

At least let's *hope* that's what the next pop idol is doing. As the demise of manufactured groups like Hear'Say and the fading away of 99 per cent of the people who were *last* year's 'next big thing' have proved, sustained live experience from regular gigging is essential for anyone who hopes to turn that 'big break' into a long-lasting career.

The range of jobs for live vocalists is enormous (we know, because Julie's done most of them!), from entertaining a rowdy audience in a pub to providing a vocal background for people who are far more interested in eating a three-course meal in a sophisticated restaurant. You might be asked to step in on vocals for a group of musicians who are playing a wedding or provide some musical interludes during a comedy or variety show, and of course, within the field of live vocalising there are a whole range of different styles you can find yourself working in, from opera to folk to jazz to hip hop.

Whatever your own style and level of vocal ability, one thing is clear: if you plan to look at the live market seriously, shyness is not an option. We'll be looking at ways to conquer nerves in later sections dealing with performance, but it's pretty impossible to predict or prepare you for everything that will happen to you during your live singing career. And maybe this is a good thing – one of the exciting things about live work is that no two gigs and no two audiences, even in the same venue, are the same.

Here's just one of Julie's early experiences as an example of what you might expect, and how it can increase your saleability as a singer:

'Back in the early days I used to sing with a rock/pop band and I got my first experience of singing in a pub at 12 o'clock in the afternoon. I didn't know people could consume so much alcohol at that time of the day! And when they started the obligatory fight we'd keep on playing. It was like something out of Blue Brothers! Mind you, regardless of the gig – i.e. a private wedding, a corporate do, a TV show – people consume a lot of alcohol and with that comes a surge of bravery. All of a sudden they're all singers and want to take the mic so they can perform a song. I usually give them the mic and most of the time it's the drink that's doing the talking. It may look easy to stand up before a club full of people waiting for you to impress them enough to down their knives and forks or drinks and applaud you, but I can assure you it's far from easy. Still, I'll always give someone their five minutes of fame – their drunken performance usually has a sobering effect. These days I'm usually the front person of a band and it's usually down to me to keep the flow and hype up the crowd or chill them out with a few ballads. If I'm 'depping' or deputising for another singer I try to find out what type of songs they usually sing and what type of audience to expect. If you're booked as a band for a gig you may work out a set list – a list of specific songs which you'll play on the night. Otherwise, I play it by ear when I get there. I *read* the crowd and call the tunes as I go along. This calls for some good musicians, ones who do a lot of sessions and gigs. They tend to know all the classics and can play them on demand. If you are playing with a band it helps if you know the key in which you sing a certain song. This'll earn you brownie points with the musicians!'

As Julie has learned the hard way, to be a successful live performer you need not just singing ability, but the ability to work with, control and *entertain* an audience. Quite often this ability can be slightly more important in the live situation than the actual quality of your vocals. We all know technically brilliant singers who are disappointing when we see them live, and most of us have listened to pub bands or 'all-round entertainers' who might not exactly have inspired us to rush out and buy their CDs but who, for the duration of a particular gig, have swept us up in their own enthusiasm and given us such a good feeling that we've ignored the bum notes, joined in the singalong at the end and possibly even shouted for an encore.

Although Julie is a pretty good singer, if we do say so ourselves, it's often her ability to *entertain* that gets her lots of 'depping' gigs – standing in for other singers who have double-booked themselves or for booked singers who have let down the venue manager at the last minute. As with any other profession, reliability is a really important factor in keeping a working singer working, and experience is the best way to establish that reliability.

For the beginning singer live performance is one of the best ways to get the experience as well as build up a personal following. It's also one of the cheapest. Even home recording requires initial financial investment, whereas if you have sufficient self-belief (and a big mouth) kick-starting a live career only involves legwork to find a venue with a stage and a microphone and then talking the venue manager into letting you loose on the paying customers. Obviously, in writing this book our goal is to get you playing decent venues and be well paid for doing it, but if you really have that burning desire to perform, the only thing stopping you starting your battle plan right now is *you*.

Of course, no matter how good you are at talking your way into a venue, your chances of ever getting asked back for a second time depend on what you deliver when you open your mouth.

If you're really serious about a singing career you'll certainly put in the practice at home, but regular live gigging helps you polish up not only your vocal skills but your entertainment skills too. That's why a residency or two, whether on a cruise ship or in a club or restaurant, is a very good goal for the aspiring live performer. It's one thing to do a great set one night, but if you have to come back the next night or the following week and perform again for the same group of people it's a great motivation for developing new material quickly or finding new things to do with existing songs. It won't be *exactly* the same audience of course – in fact, if you're any good you may well find people are starting to come along because they've been recommended to see you. Just as live gigging helps you develop your spontaneity as a performer it also builds up your sustainability. You may have sung the same song hundreds of time, but there are people in your audience who are hearing you sing it for the first time, and others who may have come just to hear your interpretation of it, so it's your job to find something new and exciting in the song every time.

Just as every audience is different every venue is different too, and you'll need to develop your ability to adapt accordingly. If you've got a big, powerful performance style this can be wonderful in larger venues, but how will you approach a smaller, more intimate space? (And smaller doesn't necessarily mean less important – you might be asked to do a private showcase for influential bookers or record-company A & R people.) Equally, what happens if your thing is gentle acoustic music and you get booked into a large hall? We can tell you from personal experience that L-shaped rooms where the performer has to work with their back to half the audience at any given time are by no means unusual around the country, as are dodgy sound systems, dodgier lighting and non-existent changing rooms. We have both played some amazing venues as well as places where the main thing that amazed us was that anyone ever thought this was a suitable performance venue in the first place.

But no matter what the circumstances, you become a seasoned performer by rising above those circumstances, and putting on a show. Live performance is without doubt the fastest way to learn to do this.

Lookalikes

As we write this, one rapidly expanding market for singers and bands is the lookalike and tribute circuit. Why pay a fortune for Robbie Williams or Celine Dion when you can have a look and sound alike version live in your own local pub? Not only can promoters gain access to the music of top live acts for a fraction of the booking fee, but Elvis, Billie Holliday and all of the top dead acts are readily available too! It has to be said from the outset that opinions on the pros and cons of this way of making a living are strongly polarised among professional musicians. It's certainly true that spending your life on stage as someone else isn't going to help you enormously in developing your own individual style. On the other hand, some lucrative lookalike work can be a big help in funding the development of your own career, and if you have major problems with stage nerves it may well be that putting on the mantle of a more experienced performer is a good way to find your feet before stepping out as yourself. We know of one established TV actress who has gained confidence in her own singing career by moonlighting as Tina Turner, and just recently we met a guitarist touring with a chart-topping sixties band, who also earns a crust as Benny in an Abba tribute band.

It's certainly true that with the right marketing a lookalike act can be very successful. A year or two ago Bjorn Again, one of the original Abba tributes, were in so much demand they had started to release singles in their own right and sell out major concert venues. It could also be argued that most of the other Abba tributes which sprung up in the wake of Bjorn Again's success were in fact tributes to a tribute band.

Currently, there must be many sixties, seventies and eighties pop stars feeling very aggrieved that while members of the public can get onto prime time TV in shows like *Stars in Your Eyes* by dressing up as them, in the current 'youth-is-everything' climate, the *real* acts themselves would have difficulty securing slots in late night cabaret shows.

Anyhow, the artistic decision of whether or not to explore the lookalike market is entirely up to you, but if you do decide to go for it, here are a couple of points to remember. We're tempted to say the first principle of becoming a lookalike act is to actually look like the person you're supposed to be paying tribute to, but we've seen enough white Tina Turners and Nat King Coles, not to mention Sikh, Chinese and female Elvises, to realise that this isn't the case. In fact, and this is good news for singers, it's the quality of the vocal that counts.

So actually, the first principle is to decide whether you make lookalike or soundalike activities simply a sideline or special feature of your own act – as singers like Sammy Davis Junior or Joe Longthorne have done with success – or whether you would like to make your living by dressing and marketing yourself as someone else. If the latter is the case, it's obviously a good idea to pick performers or groups who appeal to the party market. Abba are a very good example, as are groups like the Beatles or the Rolling Stones. Of course, if you pick a group you then have the hassle of finding other lookalike singers and musicians to complete the effect, unless the lead singer is a famous name in their own right.

It's worth keeping a close eye on the legal situation regarding lookalike and tribute acts so you don't get into trouble for 'passing off'. The usual approach is either to deliberately misspell the group name, as in The Beetles or Owaysis, or print the real artist's name in big letters ('BUDDY HOLLY LIVE TONIGHT!') with the words 'a tribute to' in very small letters elsewhere on the poster. In most cases the danger of objections comes not so much from the original artist as from rival tribute bands – there are only so many ways of misspelling popular group names.

The nature of tribute acts is that they aim to provide a 'perfect' snapshot of a group's best bits, so several years after Geri Halliwell had left the Spice Girls there were still many lookalike bands touring with a Geri clone intact.

Unlike perennial favourites like Elvis or Abba, the Spice tributes seemed to have waned in popularity along with the original group, with tributes to newer teeny bands now in demand. Career-wise it is a good idea for the lookalike act to have a few different strings to their bow. For instance, quite a few Shirley Basseys also offer Tina Turners and Chers in a sort of 'buy one get one free' arrangement. A further variation is to market yourself as a 'Tribute to the Sounds of the Seventies/Eighties/Nineties' act, in which case you can draw from the highlights of many people's careers.

Session singers and backing vocalists

Session singers

In a world currently obsessed with fame and celebrity it's worth pointing out over and over again that fame doesn't make you happy, and the music business is littered with examples of people who've learned this the hard way. Less well known are the singers and musicians who ply their trade behind the scenes at recording sessions – yet it is often they who make the most regular income from their talents, and if they are good and reliable, get as much work as they can possibly handle.

Over the years the role of the producer in the creation of music has become increasingly more important. (It always was important, of course, but in the past few decades it's quite often been the producer or DJ's name which sells a particular track more than any vocalists featured on it.) In this scenario all the elements of a piece of music, from the drums to the bass to the vocals, become just one more ingredient for the music maestro to add to the mix.

What this means for a singer is that if you have a genuinely versatile voice, or a unique vocal quality, you may be just the person a producer needs to translate the sound in their heads into aural reality. You will need to develop the mindset whereby you look at your voice as an instrument, tuning and retuning, singing the same lines over and over again until you achieve the particular effect or phrasing the producer is after.

Besides being a good source of income for the right singer, it goes without saying that session work can be an invaluable source of practical experience both in performing and recording. It can occasionally also be a route to your own time in the limelight. Trisha Yearwood was a session singer for some time, demo'ing songs for Nashville's top songwriters before finally becoming one of country music's most successful stars in her own right.

Just as in live work, Julie has found that reliability and resilience are the key factors in getting session work. Just because singers know the difference between originality and imitation doesn't mean producers do:

> 'Yes, session work can be long and laborious and you should expect the unexpected. Sometimes I've been called

to a studio session for a certain time but don't actually sing a note for hours because they're still setting up the studio, or the computer has crashed and it all needs to be reset. Then it can take hours to do something relatively simple but you're just not quite getting it. And before long you're getting frustrated with yourself. Then you get the producers who say 'sing it like Whitney' or 'Anastacia' and I'm thinking 'if you want Whitney or Anastacia go and book them for the job!' After all, I am not an impressionist – I can only sing it in my style. If they say sing it husky like Toni Braxton or ballsy like Lulu then that's fine, but it's when they ask you to sound like the person, that's when you usually have to have a word in their ear and remind them you're not *actually* Toni or Lulu. I've been in situations where the producer doesn't know exactly what they want until they hear it; and there's times when you've got two or three people instructing you on how to sing and they are all conflicting instructions (too many cooks spoiling the broth) and this can be another tedious event.

On the other hand, it can be long and productive. You might complete more than one project or at least get a guide vocal down. If you're lucky it can be short and sweet and quite painless. This is where the producer or songwriter knows what they want. You may have worked together a few times before and have a constructive working relationship. Sometimes you have to do exactly what is asked of you or you may get free rein to do whatever comes naturally to you, and possibly make an input that makes it to the final cut. You'll need to clarify your status for if and when it gets published. Some sessions require you to sign a 'buy out' form whereby you are given a one-off payment with no future claims on the track should it make it to the charts. [We'll talk about royalties, fees, etc. later on.] They may or may not have heard your voice before the actual session, so if it turns out that you're vocal isn't quite what they're looking for don't take it too personally. Just get paid for the time you were there if possible, say your goodbyes and leave!

Either way it's a great learning experience and you'll marvel at the things they can do with your voice with just the flick of a button. But be very careful what type of vocal you do in the studio. You may have to promote the song and this will undoubtedly require you to sing live and be expected to hit all the notes as per the studio recording, and the most you'll have in the way of special effects is a bit of reverb on your mike!'

Backing vocalists

The job of backing vocalist is no less finely balanced, especially during live performances. On the one hand you have to give a good professional vocal performance, but on the other hand it is not your job to outshine the person you are supposed to be backing. This can be harder than it seems: quite often the record company may have invested a lot of money in someone who while they have the 'look' may be a lot less gifted in terms of vocal ability. There's a certain degree of tweaking which can be done in the recording studio, and of course miming goes on at live shows all the time. But when the public demands live vocals, the only way to make an ordinary voice sound acceptable is to back it with the best vocalists the company can find. Far more than just 'oohs' and 'aahs', good 'BV' work can often involve singing the difficult bits along with the lead singer to disguise the fact that only one of you is actually reaching the required note.

Darlene Love, the voice of many Phil Spector hits and universally considered to be the best backing vocalist in the world, maintains that her greatest talent is 'being able to sing with anyone and make *them* sound good'. As in Darlene's case, get a reputation for being able to do this and your appointment book will start to fill up rapidly.

Also be encouraged that a really top-notch voice can never be confined to the background for very long: Darlene's 'Christmas (Baby Please Come Home)' and her other work on the legendary Phil Spector Christmas Album have become the yardstick by which all rock'n'roll Christmas songs are measured, and her face is also well know to many moviegoers from the blockbuster *Lethal Weapon* movies.

Having done her fair share of grafting as both as lead and a backing vocalist Julie maintains it's a great way to perfect your craft:

'Essentially you're there to enhance the lead vocalist. You have to blend in with harmony and their delivery of any given lyric. When there is more than one backing vocalist you have the added task of blending in with them as well as the lead. This is one of the occasions where it can get tedious (more so if they choose to record each vocalist one at time) *Tip*: Try to be the first one who lays down their vocal – then it means everyone after you has to do it *your* way. However, you may have to do the complete opposite to the lead, i.e. sing loud when they're singing soft, and vice versa. Or you may have to do a *cross vocal* – when you and the lead singer, and/or the other singers, are singing different lines at the same time and *crossing over* each other's vocal (a bit like 'London's burning, London's burning, fetch the engine, fetch the engine . . . '). My advice would be to build yourself a studio kit to take with you to all sessions. It should include things like a bottle of water, honey (and lemon if possible), throat lozenges, pen and paper, a Dictaphone – basically anything that will help you to feel comfortable should it turn out to be a long session. Dress warmly and protect your throat with a scarf or polo-neck. Studios do get hot and sticky with all that machinery around so it's probably better to wear layers so that you can strip off accordingly. You may be able to catch 40 winks while you're waiting to record so it's nice if you've got something to snuggle up in!

The other thing I'd say about studio sessions is that more often than not I'm asked to sing on a track but never get a copy of the finished product. Producers do not like to have endless copies of their 'hits' all over the place. Sometimes I'm only left with the original draft I was given to learn before the session so it's a good idea if you can take a Dictaphone with you to at least record your contribution. You may be called to redo a song a few times. It may be simply a case of tweaking your existing vocal or doing a new vocal on a different track. Allow me to clarify. If you're recording in an 8-track studio that means there are eight different tracks available for recording. Out of those, possibly three or four are dedicated to the vocalists. You may record two different vocals which both have their strengths and weak points. But the engineer or producer can select the best bits from each track and mix them together to sound like a one-off recording. You may be given this new version and told to 'live with it' for a few days with a view to re-recording it.'

Musicals

There is an ongoing debate raging in theatrical circles as to what constitutes a 'musical'. Purists argue that a musical must have both songs and story, plot and dialogue, which are inextricably linked together, and that many of the shows which currently pass for musicals are just glorified variety shows with compilations of hits by an already famous singer, group or composer, or from a particular era, merely strung together by a paper-thin plot.

From the working singer's point of view both types of show offer regular work and a chance to show off other skills such as acting or dancing. It should also be said that a necessary skill for the singer in a musical is stamina – the cast of compilation-type shows like *Smokey Joe's Cafe* or *Five Guys Named Moe* can vouch for the fact that having to sing and dance all out for two hours six nights a week and twice at weekends is no joke . . . not to mention the rigours of touring life. Even more so than being in a group, being part of a musical cast requires serious interpersonal skills, as clashes of egos coupled with the tedium of life on the road can often make what goes on backstage far more dramatic than what happens out front.

Certainly the regular performance and discipline of being in a musical can help you gain a lot of experience and stage time very quickly, but the expenditure of energy involved means your downtimes are liable to be spent either resting or trying to fit in the day-to-day necessities of life between shows (touring artists have scary mobile phone bills!). If it's very important to you to pursue your own musical direction independently of your 'bread and butter' work, attaching yourself to a musical may not be the most flexible option.

On the opposite side of the coin is the occasional dramatic production which is largely dialogue-based but which has a scene or two requiring a singer. If that singer is you, marvellous, but do remember to bring something with you to the theatre to keep you occupied. A good friend of ours was in a show which involved her waiting in the dressing room for 45 minutes of the first act, then coming on and doing her one and only number, and then having to sit back in the dressing room throughout the second half as she was required for the curtain call. Easy money some might say, but if your passion is to perform this is the kind of job which can just as easily lead to frustration.

Assuming you're not stuck in the dressing room for large amounts of time a positive by-product of musical and theatre work is that, being large affairs by their nature, musicals are complex operations which need to run smoothly to be successful. If you can establish with the director and producer that you are a team player and reliable, it's quite likely you'll be a first casting choice for subsequent productions from the same team.

A more seasonal variation of theatrical work is the pantomime circuit. As TV infiltrates this traditional medium the emphasis is switching away from dames and nursery-rhyme songs to ex-soap stars and the year's latest pop hits. Any experience you've gained dealing with rowdy pub audiences will certainly stand you in good stead when dealing with rowdy child audiences (and rowdier parents who've had to fork out for tacky merchandise and trips to the local burger joint).

In a strange way, having a competent but not spectacular singing voice can be an advantage in panto. Given that the usual cast is a combination of actors and celebrities 'having a go', generally ropey singing just adds to the panto atmosphere, whereas some directors have found that throwing a proper singer into the mix just points up the shortcomings of everybody else.

As with backing vocals, part of the art of singing in theatre is giving your best performance without deliberately upstaging everyone else – after all, you've got to live with these people during the whole run and life's a whole lot easier if you haven't turned beauty into a beast.

Singing in theatre could mean a temporary loss of your identity. If it's a character production, where you may have a costume or be totally transformed to look like someone or something else, the audience probably won't see the 'real you' until the curtain call. This is obviously different from gigs or tours when yours is the face which they actually see behind the voice. (Of course, after you've finished this book, it's our wish that your voice will speak for itself and be instantly recognisable regardless of what you're wearing.)

In America a few years ago there was even a fad for 'human jukeboxes', which consisted of large brightly painted boxes in bars, shopping malls or public parks inside of which lurked professional singers who, when paid to, would pop up and sing the song of your choice. This may not strike you as a career highlight you particularly want to aspire to, but it does demonstrate that there are as many ways to make a living from your singing as there are singers with imagination and the courage to try out new ideas.

We even know some seasoned performers who recommend busking, not so much for the spare cash as for the fact that once you can entertain a street audience you can entertain anyone. (Obviously, if you're going down this route check out the local by-laws first – we don't want you getting arrested before you've collected enough change to pay for your bail.)

From advertising jingles to voice work for animation, from singing telegrams to compèring travelling karaoke outfits, there is vocal work out there which will particularly suit both your voice and your personality, if you're prepared to put the effort into finding it. Later we'll also be looking at ways to market yourself to increase the chances of work finding *you*. But however opportunity arises, the only way of capitalising on it is by proving that when you do get the chance to perform, you are someone who can *deliver*.

And some tips on how to do that are what we'll be delivering in the next chapter.

Chapter Three

Showtime!

There's a lot of truth in the old adage 'Build a better mousetrap and the world will beat a path to your door' – or to put it another way, be the absolute best at what you do and word is inevitably going to spread. So it's a simple fact that if you want to make it as a working singer the better the show you put on the more work you are likely to be offered. Unfortunately there's no book in the world that can create that kind of excellence in a singer's performance all by itself – it's something you can only learn through trial and error and lots of practice.

But having seen many singers go through this process over the years we can certainly offer some pointers as to the best areas to focus your practising on and the elements of an act that mark the professional out from the beginner (or more to the point, from the singer who's been floundering around for years without any discernible improvement in their performance).

Breaking down your act into its individual components and then polishing each aspect until it reaches perfection is an approach that will increase your chances of success whether you are doing one or two songs in a talent contest or putting together an entire one-person show.

With each element there are several paths to excellence, and what works well for one performer may be exactly the opposite of what works for another. That's why it's important for you to experiment in each area and to look at as many other performers as you can to see what approach they take.

However, before we take a look at what you do when you get out on stage, perhaps we should take a quick look at that aspect of performance that interferes with excellence before many performers set foot on stage.

Nerves

For some it's a fluttery feeling in the stomach just before going on stage. For others it's cold sweats and bouts of retching two days before the gig. Nerves affect every performer differently, and the full-blown panic attack is just as likely to affect the singer who has been on top of the profession for 30 years as it is the first-time talent-show entrant.

So how do you get rid of nerves? Well, our first question is, are you sure you *want* to? At the root of what we call 'nerves' is our body's natural 'flight or fight' mechanism, designed to put our system on 'red alert' to cope with a crisis. In other words, our body is tuned up to perform as well as it can in whatever circumstances it finds itself. Which can be just as well. Every audience and every show is different, and in our own careers we've definitely come unstuck more often from becoming complacent and forgetting this fact than from any feelings of nervousness.

Of course, given that our nervous reaction was originally designed to get us away from rampaging dinosaurs and other such prehistoric perils, it's a bit inconvenient if it kicks in at full strength just before we go on stage at the local wine bar (not that dinosaurs and the customers of some of the bars we've played are all that dissimilar).

After all, the shakes don't exactly help microphone technique, cold sweats aren't great for a glamorous image, and hitting your top notes is a remote possibility if you can't get your vocal chords to make any sound at all.

By our nature we performers tend to overdramatise, and our attitude to the heebie jeebies is no exception. So it's worth repeating again that performance nerves are a natural feeling for every performer, and that most of the performers you admire have them just as badly as you do. If they can make it to the end of a show – not to mention to the top of the profession – regardless, then so can you.

The worst thing you can do when you're nervous is *start worrying about being nervous*, because then you'll set up a cycle that makes the whole sensation worse. Given that most of us are going to feel butterflies anyhow, it's best to change our attitude from 'Oh no, I'm nervous and that's going to make performing even harder' to 'Okay, I'm nervous, but that just means I'm more geared up to give the best show I can'.

It's worth pointing out, particularly for the beginning performer, that quite a lot of nervousness is based on the false assumption that the audience is somehow waiting for you to fail. This is very rarely the reality, even in the tougher pubs and clubs. The very fact that someone has invested time and money in coming to watch you means they have a vested interest in your being good at what you do. If you're not, your audience feels even more embarrassed than you do.

In fact, once you understand just how obsessed we humans are with ourselves to the exclusion of everything else, you'll gain another very useful insight into coping with nerves: you're the only person who really knows or cares how nervous you actually are.

When we're nervous every feeling and sensation is heightened – but only from our own perspective. In other words, when I think I'm shaking like a leaf I only seem mildly jittery to the audience. If my voice to me sounds completely out of control, it often sounds just a little bit quivery to the listener. So rather than wasting a lot of time trying *not* to be nervous, it's much more profitable to go right on being nervous and devote your energy to *disguising* that fact from the audience.

The telltale signs of nerves are usually in the breathing – short and sharp and from the upper chest – instead of the diaphragm, so the deep breathing you'll need to give a good singing performance is the same kind of breathing that helps keep nerves under control. This is another good reason to do your practise in this area.

Another indication of nerves is rapid uncontrolled movement all over the stage, in particular the inability to control flapping hands. It sounds silly but it can help a lot to imagine your feet are nailed to the floor of the stage, and if you must move your hands around, try to make a feature of it by coming up with some gestures which are appropriate to the song you are singing.

In controlling your nerves you'll also be helping your performance: one of the first goals of performance is to establish a relationship with your audience, and it's very hard to establish a relationship with someone who won't stay still for more than two seconds.

If you want to prove this principle, try to get hold of some early tapes of your favourite groups or singers. Chances are you'll see a lot of movement and careering about the stage for no good reason. Look at later performances and you'll see they've got a lot calmer and stiller, and concentrate on just singing. Yes, growing confidence plays a part in this, but simply becoming still and applying the 'fake it till you make it' principle can help even the least seasoned performer look a little more poised than they actually are.

It's also worth having a word about artificial means of dealing with nerves. All moral considerations aside, the music business is simply littered with examples of the ways in which drugs and drink may be a short-term cure for nerves but are a guaranteed ticket to disaster in every other aspect of your career.

Superstition is also a common feature of showbusiness life. It must be something to do with the basic loneliness of the profession that so many singers have lucky pins, pendants or even whole stage outfits that bring them comfort, or little rituals they always perform before going on stage. And there must be a lot of amusement in heaven at the unlikely characters who suddenly become very interested in prayer two minutes before the curtain goes up.

We're big on prayer ourselves, but we'd offer a caution when it comes to 'lucky' items and talismans, not for any religious reason but more because we've seen the chaos and misery that ensues when, inevitably, the 'magical' object gets lost or goes missing just before a really important gig.

Ultimately the best remedy for nerves is believing in your own God-given talent and your ability to cope whatever happens, and this only comes from gaining as much experience as you can, and rehearsing as much as you can before each appearance. As someone once said, rehearsing is preparing for everything you can think of that can possibly go wrong . . . so you're free to deal with confidence things that go wrong that you couldn't possibly have predicted.

Speaking of things that can't be predicted, the mark of a good show is its overall professionalism – and that's not just about what you do as a performer, it's also about how the human and technical elements of your show gel together. Even if you've never so much as changed a plug in your life, as the person on stage it's up to you to be in control of the technical appearance of your show. In the section below we'll try and shed a little light on this important area.

Lights and sound

It possibly won't come as a huge surprise to point out that in order to give a successful performance you need to be heard and seen, and that both of these operations involve electrical equipment. However, based on a lot of the acts we see, it certainly seems to be a surprise to many performers just how much difference these two elements can make to the impact of a show when handled properly.

As we've already said, it may be that the reason some beginners (and too many professionals) don't dwell on them too much is that they are viewed as 'technical' rather than 'musical', but if you are determined to make the most of your performances you need to be in control of every aspect of them.

For a start you need to get familiar with microphones and amplifiers – after all this is the basic mechanism by which your voice reaches the audience. A mike should be to a singer like a pen is to an artist or writer: something you are so much in control of that the audience shouldn't even notice it's there. Yet it's amazing how many singers get quite far into their career and still have trouble with this basic equipment, from getting tangled up in the lead, to having to stop in mid-song to adjust the stand. The solution: practice, practice and more practice . . . just don't do your practising in the middle of your performances.

If you're gigging regularly, you'll want to have your own basic microphone kit. Julie calls hers her 'handbag' equipment because it all fits in there. Although you don't need to become a fully fledged sound engineer, try to become familiar with the most common sound systems you are likely to find in pubs and clubs. Experience will show you what if any adjustments are needed to get the best results for your particular voice. (It's *your* job to know your voice, not the sound engineer's, especially if, as happens in many clubs, the 'engineer' is actually the resident DJ or even the barman.)

When you get a little more successful or a little more serious about your business, you may well decide to start investing in your own sound and lighting equipment. If you've been watching as many top live acts as you can, you'll have noticed how good sound and particularly good lighting effects can enhance the impact and 'professional' look of a performance.

Getting good quality equipment (and the right person to operate it, of course) is an investment in your career. Equally, the most expensive equipment isn't necessarily the best, so just as you would if you were buying any other technical equipment, if at all possible bring someone who knows what they're talking about along with you before you visit your local theatrical Aladdin's Cave with fast-talking sales people anxious to relieve you of your money.

Actually that's not quite fair: there are cowboys in this area as in every other area of show business, but the better equipment suppliers will usually try to give you a good deal in accordance with your budget on the basis that you may become a regular customer.

However, the best equipment in the world won't do much good if you don't use it properly, and that's as much a 'stage experience' thing as it is a technical skill.

The best place we know to have technical or artistic questions about stage lighting and sound explained in plain English is at www. makehits.com, the website of Dec Cluskey, lead singer of the chart-topping Bachelors, the original Irish boy band, and now one of the top music mentors in the business. As a singer himself, Dec's advice on marrying vocal ability to technical ability is second to none.

Your set

Throughout this book we're working with the slight handicap of knowing that every reader is not just going to have a different style, but may well be working in entirely different genres of music, from jazz to hiphop, folk to opera, and nowhere is this more obvious than in the choice of songs you choose to make up your set. However, even here there are some basic considerations which apply across the board to help you make maximum impact.

Choice of song is the most obvious one, not so much when you're doing one-hour shows or full concerts, as you then have enough time and space to demonstrate the full versatility of your range and repertoire (although even then you need to think about how you structure your show), but particularly when doing the shorter sets or even single songs which, when done well, are your 'ticket' to being let loose on more stage time and longer shows.

There are basically two kinds of song you can chose for your set: songs you like and songs you can sing well, and the two aren't necessarily the same. In particular, be wary of going for songs you enjoy singing along with whether on record or on the radio. Yes, you probably sound great doing them in the bath or in the car, but since both the vocals and the backing track for any hit song will have been expertly mixed in the studio to sound good on even the tinniest speaker, your vocal is guaranteed to sound good on top of it. It can be a completely different story when you try to sing the song all on your own to a store-bought backing track or live accompaniment. Many a talent-show entrant has come a cropper on the big night by choosing a song which sounds great in the shower but is actually miles away from their own range and key.

Even if you can sing a song really well, be careful if it's one that's been made famous by a singer of the same race, sex and general appearance as yourself, at least if you want to stand out as an individual. An obvious example might be if you are a black female vocalist doing a song made famous by Aretha Franklin. You can give the best performance ever, but either you'll end up being compared unfavourably to Aretha, or if the song goes down really well it'll be Aretha they're clapping not you.

Of course, for party or wedding gigs, the more classic and recognisable songs you include, the better.

Even if you are choosing from the back catalogues of well-known artists and from the greatest hits of popular eras – and in many commercial gigs from restaurants to cabarets to weddings it's part of your job to sing those songs – try to be a little creative in your choices. By all means do the big number one hits, but try to occasionally throw in a song or two that people remember but that doesn't get trotted out quite so often. A day or two of listening to the 'classic hits' type radio stations should suggest a couple of good examples. There's nothing like the ripple of delighted applause and recognition as you launch into the opening bars of an 'oldie but goldie' to raise your confidence level, and all the more so if it's a song people are rediscovering through *you* rather than one they've heard done to death every other day of the week.

A very good tack is to choose well-known songs by artists of the opposite sex to yourself (apologies if you're a drag act). You can do an almost note-for-note cover of a big hit song, but if you're singing something in a male voice that people usually hear sung by a female, or vice versa, it can sound fresh, exciting and new, and no matter how accomplished the original vocal, your version won't suffer from unfair comparison.

Make sure the subject matter of the song transfers, of course. Candi Staton's 'Young Hearts Run Free' is probably one of the most famous songs of the entire disco era, and almost always gets an enthusiastic reaction from audiences on the first few bars, even if the vocalist doesn't happen to have Candi's unique voice – but a male singer would need to do quite a lot of lyrical adaptation to tell the story of a 'lost and lonely wife'. For that matter, given that the song was written about Candi's own turbulent life, even female singers in their teens or early twenties might have difficulty delivering it with the required conviction if they haven't had comparable experiences.

It's not that you need to have lived every situation in every song you sing, but like a method actor, you need to find something 'real' for yourself in each song to communicate the lyrics as more than just words. There are enough great country songs out there so it shouldn't be too difficult to choose one which doesn't contain references to Texas, Nashville or Tennessee if you're a singer who quite obviously hasn't been too far outside Cricklewood.

While we're on the subject, do take the time to work out the actual words of the song you are singing. In our resource section you'll find a number of websites which will help you discover lyrics for most songs you may want to include in your act. There are also a whole host of other popular websites which revel in our ability to mishear and mispronounce song lyrics. For instance, the classic Jimi Hendrix track 'Excuse Me While I Kiss the Sky' has apparently been mangled as 'Excuse Me While I Kiss this Guy'.

If you do a novelty act you can have fun with lyrics of course – even Elvis wasn't above messing about with 'Are You Lonesome Tonight' ('Does Your Hair Look a Fright?'). But just make sure the audience are laughing *with* you, not at you.

Many sixties and seventies soul songs refer to 'working for The Man', a phrase which has lots of resonance in terms of the civil rights struggle and social and cultural history. Younger singers, both black and white, often mistakenly sing about 'working for *a* man', which doesn't have the same resonance at all.

On the subject of history, just as taking a song across the male/female divide can give it a unique flavour, taking a song from a different style of music from the one you are working in can make it a highlight of your act, be it a jazz number sung in country style or a disco classic given a folky delivery. It's surprising how many uptempo songs can have quite dark lyrics, and giving them a slower ballad delivery can often bring this out and show off your own vocal strengths to boot. On the other hand, giving a ballad an uptempo flavour can really wake up an audience.

For the working singer, it obviously makes sense to expand your repertoire with an eye to being able to fulfil as many types of engagement as possible. Quite often customers booking you for specific gigs will specify the songs they want you to perform, and the ones which get asked for most frequently are the ones which will become the staples of your set. (There will be the occasional 'classic', of course, which you either won't be able to perform particularly well or just plain can't stand, in which case do try to come up with an alternative in the same tempo or style.)

Aim for a good basic mix of uptempo and slower numbers, and practise putting them together to form a balanced set. A good basic formula is to start off with something bouncy and catchy to get the audience on side, then slow things down with a ballad or two, then bring the tempo back up for a big finish.

Conversely, if you're doing a supper club a generally slow and relaxed set may be best, as people may not necessarily want to eat their dinner with you belting out a medley of the Sex Pistols' greatest hits in their ears.

It can certainly make a set more personal if you occasionally introduce 'a song that means a lot to me' with an appropriate story, but as a working singer your job is to entertain the customers rather than yourself, so try not to be too 'anoraky' in your musical choices.

Obviously in all of the above we have assumed you are doing cover versions and popular songs. But even if you are a singer–songwriter we would suggest a cover version or two, particularly at the beginning of your set as it is a very effective way of getting an audience 'tuned in' to your voice.

Even if you are doing entirely original songs, the same basic rules about planning your set apply. What songs are the most accessible or have the most impact to start off with? What would be a good strong song to finish with? You can be a little too close to songs you have written yourself so you may want to get some objective opinions before answering these questions.

Whether doing covers or originals, be wary of doing several songs back to back which, although strong in their own right, sound very similar in tempo or lyrical content. On a more practical note, have a slower song or two on hand even if most of your set is uptempo numbers – you may want to create a little space for both you and the audience to catch your breath.

Lastly, even if your set is only three songs, do have a fourth one up your sleeve for an encore. It's surprising how many singers get called back and are caught by surprise, ending up having to do one of their original songs all over again.

The more performances you do, the more you'll start to get a feel for which songs and which sets go down best with different audiences. If you do a lot of weddings, part of your job is to get people up dancing, and you and your band need to have a good selection of 'floor fillers' at your disposal, preferably from as many different eras as possible, to cater for everyone from jiving grandads to teeny boy band followers.

In a supper club, on the other hand, you may lean towards slower, more soulful numbers, although you still need to sing pretty powerfully to avoid being drowned out by the sound of people munching and clinking cutlery.

In any public function, and sometimes even during your own show, you may get the audience shouting out requests or handing up song titles on folded pieces of paper. This is a good sign as it shows the crowd likes what you are doing, but even if you do know the requested songs and can sing them well, ration your performance to a couple of requests and stick to your basic set.

Remember: the goal of a performance is to remain in control and entertain everyone in the audience, not just the noisier or more upfront punters.

Obviously, if you get the same request handed up time and time again it may pay you to learn the song in question. It may also be that the songs suggested are deliberately incongruous with the rest of your act – for instance, tipsy audience members often think it is a great wheeze to request that cabaret or classical-style singers do a Clash or Eminem song. (Of course, if you can surprise them and do a version in your own style you'll win a lot of respect. In fact it's not unknown for a singer to have a prepared 'unusual request' hidden away for just such a purpose.)

Handwritten requests can be difficult to decipher at the best of times, and there is a well-known story about an Irish band in New York who kept getting asked for a song called 'Paddy, Me Boy'. After much head-scratching they finally asked the punter to sing it for them. He took a deep breath and warbled 'Paddy Me Boy . . . is that the Chattanooga choo choo'.

Audience interaction

Requests aside, audience interaction is an area that many singers find the most difficult. Which is a shame because it's establishing a good rapport with an audience that really makes your act stand out.

Remember again the basic principle that most audiences want you to do well and be in control (if you're playing too many gigs with the other sort of audience, you may well want to take a closer look at your vision and marketing strategy).

There's a basic principle that control isn't *given*, it's *taken*, and you will see many performers in and out of the music world use this to their advantage at the start of their act. If you've chosen your opening number (or numbers) carefully and you can sing well, you'll already have got audience attention. But after the first or second song make a point of getting the audience to *do something* at your command.

It doesn't need to be anything too difficult. Just getting them to answer a question will do 'Anyone here from (name of the place you're in)' is a standard opener. Rappers often get 'everyone in the house' to shout 'Yo!', which is exactly the same principle.

In some strange Pavlovian way, once you can get a group of people to do something because you told them to, you have control over them, at least temporarily.

Don't overdo it, though – they don't know you well and even though they're sitting in the dark, can still be much more self-conscious than you might think. Asking people to clap their hands or stand up and dance too early in your set can be counterproductive – if they *don't* do what you ask them to, you've just demonstrated that you're *not* in control.

As your act progresses and you gain more experience you'll learn to 'work' an audience, to feel when they're tiring or when they're ready to be taken to the next level. After each show you may want to make adjustments to your set when you feel a fast song or a slower song might have worked better at a certain point. Really experienced singers (with really forgiving bands) may well change the set in mid-show if they feel something will work better with a particular audience.

Once you do get the audience on your side you can really start to make the show interactive – the difference between a 'singer' and an 'entertainer' could be expressed as the fact that a singer wants to show people how well they can sing, while an entertainer wants to use their singing and other abilities to give the audience the time of their lives. How many times have you seen a really big star close a great show with their biggest hit record . . . and turn the microphone out towards the audience, so they can sing the chorus. When it works it's magic, and mostly all it takes is the confidence to take charge and make the show about the audience rather than about you. (Of course, we're not suggesting you can get the audience to do the whole gig for you, you'll need to have given them their money's worth by singing a bit yourself, first.)

While it's important to be in control of your audience, it's also important not to come across as arrogant or full of yourself – honesty and even a little vulnerability (which is different from sloppiness) can win people over, too.

It's professional to remember the lyrics of songs you are singing, but it's also human to forget them every so often. You can make two choices when this or a similar mishap occurs on stage: either you plough on in 'show must go on' mode or you make a joke of it. It doesn't have to be a particularly funny joke, either. You can make up some nonsense lyrics for the song, or ask the audience how the rest of it goes, or you can have some stock lines ready when the microphone stand falls over ('That's the last time I borrow a mike from Aeroflot'), but coping with the situation rather than storming off stage in a strop will win you brownie points with any audience and may even be one of the highlights of the evening.

And yes, you will get the occasional heckler who shouts out something in the middle of a slow song, or generally makes a nuisance of themselves. In most cases the thing to bear in mind is that *you* have the microphone so you are in control. Most audiences are on your side and if you can think of something even vaguely amusing to reply to the heckler you'll get a clap (again there are plenty of stock lines you can use – you'll gather lots from any given night at your local comedy club). Staying relaxed is the key. There is a world of difference between heckling and somebody shouting out something witty which actually adds to your show – if you think what they said was funny laugh along with everyone else. You may even want to repeat the line for those who didn't hear it.

Julie, being the glamorous lady that she is, sometimes finds males getting a little too noisy during her set, and has been known to bear down on them with the microphone and sing the rest of the song directly to them (instantly transforming them into embarrassed little boys). It's a confidence thing: if you're not quite at that level yet you can simply plough on with the song, but whatever you do, don't let hecklers 'get' to you. In any decent kind of venue the management should be keeping an eye out and removing anyone who gets really disruptive. (If you haven't reached that level of venue yet, just keep smiling and remember that what doesn't kill you makes you stronger.)

Heckling doesn't have to be just from humans, of course – despite all the warnings and pre-show announcements, there's always the possibility that a mobile phone or pager will start going off in the middle of your big ballad. Again, depending on how you handle it, this can be an irritation or an opportunity. Howard Hewett, the golden-voiced lead singer of soul group Shalamar, has been known to deal with this by sweeping the offending phone from the audience member's hand, and serenading the surprised caller.

We're not suggesting, by the way, that every singer needs to be a comedian. It's perfectly possible to run through your entire set without saying a word to the audience, and if you have a good enough set you may even pull that off. It's just that we have found from our own experience that getting practice interacting with the audience gives you a lot more flexibility. But it's a matter of balance. A few words or a funny story at the beginning of a song can set the scene and make the music that follows much more personal and meaningful, but do try to avoid boring the audience with long rambling intros when it's music they have paid to see. (Or if your intros are getting a better reaction than your songs you could always do a Billy Connolly and drop the music altogether.)

Stage presence

Live performance is about more than just words and music, it is about convincing the audience that they are in the presence of a *star*. The only way to do that is to convince *yourself* that you are a star from the moment you embark on your singing career.

We've already talked about 'faking confidence till you make it' in relation to coping with nerves, and the same thing applies to your general image and visual presentation. You don't prove you are a star when you begin to sing – you prove you are a star from the moment the audience sets eyes on you. How do you come on stage? Nervous, needy of attention or confident in your talent and ability, looking like you and the audience are going to have a good time?

Watch videos of stars you admire and focus on their own stage entrances. There are quite a few different ways of establishing confidence and control, and you may have to try a few different ones to discover the one that works best for you.

For instance, some singers and groups adopt a high-energy approach, with tight, exciting choreography enhanced by light, sound and special effects. If that seems a little outside your budget, reflect on how many big stars – who could well afford the full range of bells and whistles – instead opt for a simple, dramatic entrance, maybe just standing still and silhouetted for a moment, ready to launch into a powerful vocal when the applause dies down.

We've already mentioned the power of stillness on stage, but obviously the degree to which you move about depends on your particular act and the style of music you are working in, so perhaps the general rule is that if you are going to move around on stage, make sure you move for a reason. One of the most common signals of a beginning singer is aimless shuffling about, waving hands around for no good reason.

Compare that with more seasoned performers who may well use their hands to 'illustrate' song lyrics, but always in a way that's thought out and matches or complements what they are singing about. Equally, a good performer will use the stage area to the maximum – not too much and not all at once, but smoothly covering each angle of the room and making (or faking) eye contact with every section of the audience so that every part of the crowd is made to feel that the show is being performed to them.

Legendary singing groups like the Supremes or the Three Degrees used to practise their movements in front of full-length mirrors almost as much as they practised their vocals, while Garth Brooks became the first country music star to seriously pack out rock-sized stadiums by adopting a simple principle of performance. Before each show he is said to have sought out 'the worst seat in the house' and then designed his show to entertain the person sitting in that seat to the maximum, on the basis that if the person in the worst seat thought his show was good, everyone else in the theatre would think it was fantastic.

The 'sit in your own audience' principle is a valuable one even if you're not doing stadium-sized gigs as yet. For instance, do you need to make your movements bigger or address more of your pre-song patter to the back of the hall? Since you can't physically be in two places at once, it can be really useful to have a trusted friend sit in on one of your shows and report back to you what they *actually* saw and heard, not what you *intended* them to see and hear or what you *thought* the audience saw and heard. If there's a difference between those various versions of your show you may need to see how you can adjust it accordingly.

Image

As the visual aspect of your stage act is so important you need to have a think about your image. Even if you've never addressed this aspect of your act before, you already have an image – even if it's 'Never heard of you' or 'Look what the cat dragged in'. If that's not quite the image that you want, you need to put some work into changing it . Depending on the kind of music you sing there may already be specific parameters for the required image, whether it's jeans for rock bands or sequinned dresses for cabaret singers, but even then you need to adapt the image in some way that is unique to you.

Avoid therefore the tendency to copy the image of another singer, no matter how successful they are or how much you admire them. Chances are their stylist has designed that image specifically for them and it won't look as good on you. More to the point, if the singer really is on the cutting edge they will already have moved on and adopted a whole new image while various imitators are ripping off their old one.

Bear in mind that your stage image is just that – designed to be viewed on a stage. So just as you need to double-check the message that you are sending in your stage act, you need to double-check whatever image you are putting across as well. Not all of the clothes we enjoy wearing are the ones which flatter us or suit us best, and the same goes for hairstyles and make-up.

Get a cross-section of responses from as many people as possible to see how your image is developing. Does the look you fondly imagine is 'mean and moody' actually say 'sad and grumpy' or does your 'sexy' image actually say 'desperate'?

It's particularly important for female performers to be confident in their image because believe us, you are going to get a lot of comments about it, whether asked for or not, and it also has to be admitted that sometimes female members of the audience can be your toughest critics.

Sadly, we feel the need to point out that a 'star image' is also about less creative elements such as cleanliness and grooming – something many performers don't seem to pay nearly enough attention to. The nature of being a performer is that you are constantly on show, and often under bright lights guaranteed to show up the slightest flaw or imperfection. That means that moisturising your face, manicuring your nails, and keeping your hair in good condition are all part of the job, not luxuries to get around to when you have the time or money. (And this especially means *you*, male performers!)

The same applies when you are off stage. You may not have your full stage gear on, but you still need to create the star impression by standing out from the crowd for the right reasons.

Even in the Punk era, much of the 'anarchy' was heavily styled by designers like Vivienne Westwood, and even the wildest rock band needs to understand the difference between 'scruffy and rebellious' and 'smelly and dirty'.

We've spent most of this chapter concentrating on things you need to keep in mind when you're on stage – be that stage in the corner of a pub, on the deck of cruise ship or in a major concert venue. Being able to deliver the goods live is the best plank to build a working career on, not just because in an emergency you could earn a crust by busking, but also because making an impression live can often lead to other, sometimes even more lucrative, job offers.

While much of the stuff we've already discussed is relevant no matter what performance situation you find yourself in, there are two types of performance which need special mention for diametrically opposite reasons. Recording, for obvious reasons, removes everything that visual style can add to your work, and is the area where your vocal ability on its own comes to the fore (hence the notorious tendency of manufactured bands to mime to vocals which are actually the work of session singers).

TV work, by contrast, places the emphasis squarely on your visual abilities. As a seasoned session and backing singer Julie has had a lot of experience of both these situations. First let's take a look (or should we say a listen) to her observations on recording.

Recording sessions

'I think I've experienced a variety of them and then some – from a little four-track set-up in someone's bedroom where I had to sing into one earpiece of a pair of headphones which were stuffed with loo paper and held together with gaffer tape, to the very latest state-of-the-art, highest of hi-tech studios with mixing desks resembling something aboard the Starship Enterprise with buttons that slide up and down on their own – very eerie but fascinating to watch!

It really depends on the client and their budget. You may find that at the beginning of your career you'll be doing a lot of the 'bedroom' sessions (musically speaking), as when you start networking you'll probably come across wannabe producers who need to get a demo vocal on a track. You probably won't get paid for the session as you are both hoping for bigger things down the line. But you should ensure that you get a copy of everything you do. So go to the session armed with a blank cassette, minidisc or CD and don't be afraid to ask what happens if the track picks up some outside interest – i.e. what percentage of the royalties you could expect, especially if you've contributed to the melody and lyrics. [Check our chapter on the business of music later in the book for many more reasons why prior agreements are important – often even more so when there is no hard cash involved.]

Don't get me wrong – some people have great home-recording facilities where a spare room or garage has been professionally converted into a studio. It tends to be more economical to do all the pre-production work 'at home' and to book a decent studio for the final mixes.

You may have the good fortune to work in a studio that has its own restaurant, TV lounge and games room, but you should still have your survival kit nearby and you may even bump into a famous recording artist at work. Just check out the vibe first – they may not be in the mood to greet fans or sign autographs, as they will be dressed for comfort not glamour. Whether it's the right time to pitch your own demo to them is up to you and your level of self-confidence to decide.

Where you actually record can vary according to the layout of the studio. You could be in the same room as the engineer, or in another room where you can't see the studio audience, or maybe like a goldfish – in a soundproof room with windows so that you can see everyone and they can see you!

If you're a bit conscious of the gurning you may have to do to squeeze those difficult notes out then you can draw the curtains (if they have them) or stick the lyrics up in front of you.

Everything should be set up for you to sing. Most studios insist that you ask the engineer to make any adjustments to the equipment, especially when it comes to the 'million dollar' microphone they use. You'll also get a pair of headphones – aka 'cans' – and the sound can be adjusted to suit your needs. It is the norm to wear one can directly over one ear and the other just behind the ear, allowing you to hear your raw vocal and anyone else who may be in the booth with you.

Some studios and record labels employ session singers to lay down guide vocals for a track that may be sold to an existing pop star as a potential single or album release. For this you'll probably be paid a 'buy out' fee and you'll have to sign a form accepting this payment as a final payment. That's great if the track is never used but if it is, and even if it sells thousands, you won't be able to claim an extra penny. More often than not, you'll be given a lyric sheet and told exactly how to sing each line, but there may be an occasion where you are given total vocal freedom to interpret the song as you feel it, and if that is the case make sure your contribution is acknowledged in writing.

Occasionally, I strike it lucky with a one-off vocal and I'm in and out within the hour. But there have been times where I've been in a studio for 24 hours plus. It could be a simple phrase that I'm not getting right or, in a group situation, it might be one of the other vocalists who can't get it together on her designated parts, subsequently delaying the other vocals. If it's your turn to have the studio session from hell, try to relax. Breathe deeply. Lubricate and rest your voice for a while. Look at other ways you could deliver the phrase. Or it could be that you're singing flat (below the intended note) or sharp (above the note). One of the other singers may end up doing it but this is no reflection on your performance. It could simply be that the line suits her voice better.

Once you're on the circuit you'll no doubt get to know other singers and even work alongside them. A lot of work can come directly from other singers so make sure you're pleasant to work with. I'm lucky to have worked with singers who are good friends as well as good vocalists. We each know which note the other will go to, i.e. top, melody or bottom, and generally work very efficiently.

I usually involve myself in the recording of the vocals but don't hang around for the mixing stages. After a long session the last thing I want is to hang around whilst the engineer records a good mix. Relationships can suffer if your partner isn't very supportive and doesn't understand 'why it takes so long'. There are loads of hi-tech studio facilities which can make everyone's life easier. If you're struggling with a note the pitch can be adjusted to suit you and then returned to normal afterwards. Choruses can be sung once and then copied and pasted into the chorus positions throughout the track.

If you are very much into your own music and performance the 'stop-start' nature of recording can be quite frustrating – and that's just working on your own tracks. When you're toiling away anonymously for hours to make another producer or perhaps a 'soap star turned pop star' look good the whole process may be more than the ego can bear. But if you don't have those ego or patience problems, and are prepared to put in the effort to get phrases and effects right no matter how many 'takes' it requires, your reputation among producers and fellow musicians can end up getting you a lot of recording work, useful not just for your own finances but also for giving you vital experience you can use when it's *your* time to take the lead microphone.'

TV gigs

Julie has mustered up a great selection of fun memories through TV work over the years.

'I got treated like royalty and I was only the backing singer. It usually means days of rehearsal and preparation for just three and a half minutes of fame on the silver screen. You'll be taken shopping for clothes and shoes (depending on the budget, which will depend on the artist you're backing), or a stylist might bring a rail of clothes for you to choose from. Sometimes you get to keep the gear, which is a great bonus.

Everything from hair to make-up needs to be particularly flawless for TV gigs. [We've already mentioned the importance of image.] Each show usually has its own team of professionals, although an artist may have their own personal team as part of their entourage to create a specific look to compliment the track.

On the day itself, there'll be cameramen, gaffers, light and sound engineers, floor managers and a zillion other personnel all needing to rehearse their parts. You'll be called when you're needed and time is very much of the essence – most of the personnel belong to a union and will not go beyond a designated finishing time. So you have to make sure you're in the right place at the right time. There's usually someone who has the task of ensuring everyone is on time for everything, and that's the road manager. You usually have one or two dry runs, plus one dress rehearsal (in full costume and make-up) before the actual recording. If it's a live show – like one of the Saturday morning kiddies' shows – you'll have just one chance to get it right. However, if it's a pre-recorded show for future broadcast you might get a chance to do it again if you mess it up. The main focus will obviously be on the lead singer, but you shouldn't let your performance slip for one second because you never know when one of the many cameras are recording you!

If you're lucky enough to be working with a current chart-topping artist you can enjoy some of the luxuries involved. They can include a chauffeur-driven car to pick you up and drop you off. I remember working with Soul II Soul and getting the driver to deliberately toot the horn loudly so that the neighbours would look out and see yours truly stepping into a shiny black luxury Jaguar – sad, but true and definitely something I could get used to!

Get friends or family to videotape the programme for you – not only are videos a nice memory of your five minutes of fame, they can also act as a demo or showreel [see the chapter on marketing coming up shortly]. Above all, they are good for critical analysis – maybe you were grinning a bit too much or you had your eyes shut for most of the time, or there was something else you could improve on for the next performance.

I'm not a person who gets star-struck but it is always nice to see a celebrity and discover how down-to-earth they are. Sir Bob Geldof and James Brown are two artists that spring to mind, and more recently the Sugababes were really sweet to meet. I also remember Take That being at a *Top of the Pops* recording and how much fun they were. I get autographs for friends and family, who now have an impressive selection of famous signatures. Funny how they never ask for mine!'

As we said at the beginning of the chapter, the secret of good performance is to take responsibility for every aspect of it yourself and work on bringing every element of your show up to the highest standard you can. Having said that, for most singers there will be occasions where it's not just your performance you have to worry about, but also integrating that performance with the efforts of other people to produce a satisfying whole. If you happen to be a singer with a group or a band, this cooperation may become a major element of your career, and as you and your outfit practise and get to know each other better, as with Julie and her colleagues in the session business, you can develop a real tightness and communal approach – all the best bands and groups are successful way beyond the sum of their parts. However, the nature of being a working singer is that you'll frequently be working with musicians and bands you may never have worked with before (and may never see again). How do you perform with these unknown quantities in a way that will result in harmony both on stage and off? As you'll see from Julie's advice below, knowing your own performance style inside out is a very good first step.

Working with musicians

'Walk into a venue where they advertise 'live music' and you'll probably find that the only thing that's live is the singer! All the instruments are pre-recorded onto backing tracks – sort of like a karaoke set-up but without the TV monitor. Most proprietors only have a general entertainments licence which can cover a maximum of two people performing. Any more than this constitutes a band and a special licence is required. These 'duo' gigs are cool although they don't leave much room to be flexible. The tracks usually sound as close to the real thing as possible and tend to go down well with the audience, who recognise them straight away. Some come complete with backing vocals (BVs), making life for the lead singer a little easier. But because the tracks are pre-recorded you can't extend them, or shorten them, or do anything but stick to the format – not much chance to develop your audience-rapport skills!

Working with musicians is totally different. The vibe is so tangible – especially when you're all 'on the one'. I've worked with various line-ups, from a trio to a 30-piece big band, and nothing can beat the buzz of real musicians jamming on a track. A standard radio-edited track (usually three-and-a-half minutes) can be extended to 10 minutes if the vibe demands it. And even though there's a designated musical director (MD) you can 'conduct the band', calling on any one of them to do a solo, or to take it down, pick it up, or in the words of the Godfather of Soul, 'take it to the bridge'.

Most musicians are serious musos who can read music and have a good ear – almost bionic in some cases – that can hear when you're singing flat or sharp! They tend to look down their noses at us singers because we don't play instruments, but I always remind them that my voice is an instrument too and needs just as much TLC, tuning and protection as their bit of brass or kit. When working with musicians it helps if you know what keys you do particular songs in. If you're going to do it in the original key, as recorded by the original artist, fine, but if you need it in a different key try to know which one instead of saying 'higher' or 'lower'! I tend to change the key if I'm singing a song recorded by a male artist. There is a gadget called a pitch pipe used by guitarists for tuning their instruments, but some singers use it to tune their voices. This is particularly useful if you're doing an a cappella song or where the vocal is the first sound of a track and the band doesn't kick in till the second verse (like the Lauryn Hill version of 'Killing Me Softly').

There are a lot of multi-talented musicians out there who can sing as well as play instruments. I've done some gigs with a keyboard player/singer, saxophonist/singer, guitarist/singer, etc., and these are great because it means they can share the load and allow you to rest your voice while they're singing.'

If you get the bug for working with live music you could always go the whole hog and learn an instrument yourself. Whether it's keyboards or guitar, don't believe the myth that you're too old to pick up something new – like any other aspect of your career, if you're determined enough you'll put in the time and effort required to succeed (after all, Robert De Niro reportedly learned to play saxophone purely for his role in *New York, New York*). Go back over our first chapter on singing teachers and apply the same principle to finding a good music teachers. Be aware though, that singing and playing are two different functions, and even after your newly acquired instrumental skills have reached a performance level it may take some further work to be able to do both with style and grace. You may want to make your initial goal simply to perform one song with your own accompaniment towards the end of your set, before you launch into full sound and vision concerts.

Every artist, be they actor, singer or musician, should be aiming to build up a self-contained show lasting an hour or more. Once you've got something that works, not only can you seek slots on other people's stages and bills, you can also start marketing your own products to small theatres, festivals and anywhere else you can find people looking for a good evening out. If you also have CDs and other merchandise to sell at these events, and are prepared to put some time into marketing the whole package, a lucrative and regular income is a real possibility. You can check out our website www.webtoonist.com for detailed step-by-step information on putting together a show, but be encouraged that even if you are just beginning the process of building your act, polishing and changing it as you gain more experience, you are already building a firm foundation for a quality show of your own.

In fact, in whatever direction you take your performances, you should be constantly trying out new approaches and elements to keep your live act 'live'. Not everything is going to work, which is why it's important to place any new material in a part of your set where the audience is already well warmed up by stuff you know works – and where you have other stuff that you know works following in case things don't go according to plan.

As we said at the beginning of this chapter, a good performer never stops learning and developing, and there is a lifetime to be spent polishing your performance style. Of course, before you get onto your own stage or in your own show you are going to have to prove yourself on many other stages and in other people's shows to begin with.

In the next chapter we'll do our best to equip you to travel on the road to establishing yourself at the fastest speed possible.

Chapter Four

If They Could See Me Now . . .

Talent contests and auditions

Once you know that your performance works, it's time to really pursue the goal of being a working singer. Of course your ultimate goal is to have all your work come by 'word of mouth' – that golden day when all over the world there are movers and shakers in show business who don't just want a singer, they want *you* – but until that day comes there are basically two ways of getting singing work. One way is to generate work for yourself, and to this end we have a whole chapter on marketing later in the book.

The other way, and the one through which it is easiest to kick-start your career, is via talent contests, auditions for solo spots or shows, and basically by turning up for any event you find out about that requires a singer with the aim of convincing them that *you* are the singer they are looking for.

Inevitably, turning up for contests and auditions means that you are also going to be turned *down* at lots of contests and auditions. Just as every singer has individual talent, so every potential employer is looking for different things, some of which you may be able to provide and some of which you won't.

It may also be the case that you aren't experienced enough as yet to be chosen at a particular audition, but look at it this way: just turning up for the audition is a major step towards increasing your experience.

The first thing to say is that there is no golden rule that will guarantee success in every audition or competition, and this is true whether you are a complete beginner or an established star. A friend of ours, who happens to be as big a star as they come, was on holiday some years ago and was persuaded to enter a karaoke competition in her hotel. She duly performed her own million-selling hit single – and came third.

However, in both talent contests and auditions, following some basic rules will greatly increase your chances of success.

Talent contests

Talent contests are probably the easiest and quickest way to get your act in front of a paying audience (even if they get in free and are only paying for drinks at the bar). 'Search for a Star' type shows operate on a wide range of levels, from 'amateur night' down the local pub to national contests with regional heats, grand finals, and sometimes very impressive prizes ranging from holidays and large cheques to recording contracts and career development.

As there has been a shift away from 'variety' style entertainment in the past few decades you are just as likely to find professional and semi-professional performers throwing their hats into the ring at these contests as you are complete beginners.

It's quite common to find that aspiring singers travel from long distances to appear on these showcases, and although almost anyone who applies and can afford the entry fee will get their chance to perform, don't be disappointed if you find there's already a long waiting list when you phone up.

Actually, this high demand for places is all to the good. In the old days the club circuit was the training ground for up-and-coming singers, who improved their skills not just through the extra experience gained at every gig but also simply by watching how the old pros did it when they closed the show. Now talent contests perform the same function, with the added incentive that with an individual approach, the wind in your sails and the right judging panel, a relative beginner might just sneak past more experienced acts in a competition and win the day.

Legend has it that jazz diva Ella Fitzgerald got her first big break in a talent contest for which she wasn't even entered: apparently she only turned up to support a friend who was taking part, and when the friend got cold feet Ella stepped in, taking the big prize (not to mention Manhattan, The Bronx and Staten Island too).

One advantage of being a little way down the waiting list is that, if you're prone to cold feet and the talent contest you've entered for is holding several heats, it makes a lot of sense to try to get along to one of the heats before the one you're actually entered in. It will give you a very good idea of the format of the contest, the standard of the acts and the kind of audience you can expect.

If the talent contest is for singers only, try to get a feel for the range of music represented.

A few years ago the R & B girl group TLC was very much in vogue, so that the majority of entrants to any inner city singers' showcase were similar groups of three or four girls, or solo girl singers who looked like they could be slotted into one of those groups at the drop of a hat. In between these acts were other singers, male and female, singing in styles ranging from folk to blues, but inevitably the winners, whether by audience vote or judge's decision, would be TLC clones.

Was this disappointing for the other singers on the bill? Probably. Was it a waste of time their entering the competition? Not at all. What most beginners who refuse to enter talent contests tell us is 'I don't believe in competition'. What they really mean is 'Losing would be too big a blow to my confidence'. The truth is if you've got a 'winner's mentality' you never even consider the possibility of losing, but even if you don't come first you're tough enough to pick yourself up, dust yourself off and start all over again.

Not every audience you perform to is going to have the same taste in music as you anyhow, and you might just surprise yourself and them if you give it your best shot.

If you do get to an early heat of the contest, try to put yourself in the mind of a judge watching the other singers. What do they do that impresses you, whether in attitude, dress or vocal style? Is there anything you can learn and apply to your own act?

Equally, what do other acts do that annoys you? Maybe they don't make eye contact with anyone outside the first row of the audience. Or do they perform their entire act to the judges and ignore everyone else in the room (guaranteed to annoy everyone, *including* the judges if they have any knowledge of stage craft).

Don't just focus on singers who are vaguely similar to you: male singers can learn from females, and R & B divas from country and western bands.

Put a little practice time in after you've finished your research expedition and see if you can incorporate the good stuff you learned into your own act – and more importantly avoid making some of the obvious mistakes.

The Bible tells us to 'cast out the log in your own eye before you deal with the speck in your neighbour's', and it's a basic truism that most of the errors that annoy us most in others are ones which we make in some form or another ourselves.

Did you feel the performer was ignoring you at any point in their act? Now think about your own act: is there any point when people on one or other side of the hall might feel you are ignoring *them*? If so, and given that you can't be in two places at once, what do you do about it? For the answer find a video of any major star doing a concert 'in the round' and watch how they make sure every side of the room is 'covered'.

Not that we're encouraging you to make the error of lifting chunks of people's acts wholesale to use in your own. This used to be a common activity of stand-up comedians who worked the clubs, but has died down somewhat – not so much from a sweeping outbreak of honesty as because modern comedians tend to tailor their material to their own specific personalities. However, that's not to say that some hoary old jokes don't turn up in 'cutting edge' comedy routines, cleverly adapted to match new topics and approaches.

You can apply much the same principle to a musical act: if a singer introduces a song from an interesting angle, has a neat way of getting the audience involved or comes up with a classy vocal effect, you'll find that even if you put your scruples aside and just copy it, the end result is never as good as the original (especially if you're crazy enough to do it in front of the judges who saw the originator do it at the previous heat!).

A much better way is to try to analyse *why* this element of the act works. Is it because the intro links a song to personal experience? Does the performer make audience participation fun rather than just snapping out orders for everyone to 'clap along?'

Now see if you can blend a similar approach into your existing act but in a way that suits *your* stage persona.

Vonda Shepherd, the singer from the Ally McBeal TV show, says she first wanted to become a musician from listening to the 'Sweetheart of Soul', Candi Staton on the radio. R & B Diva Mary J. Blige has also expressed admiration for Candi. You wouldn't confuse any of these three singers with one another if you heard or saw them, but listen to their performances and it's not hard to spot the heartfelt passion and 'realness' that both Mary and Vonda have picked up from Candi and carried on in their own styles.

One question we're often asked about talent contests is 'Where in the running order is best to go on?' You may not be given the choice or it may be that whichever act turns up first gets to pick their place in the running order. In a variety-style show, the organisers may well adjust the running order to slot in comedians and other speciality acts between every two singers, which is a good thing for all concerned.

But if you *do* get the chance to choose where you go on the bill, take our advice that there is one spot you should *always* pick to guarantee your success. What is that spot? The one *you* are most comfortable with.

Yes, despite all the horror stories we hear about going on first or going on after the interval, we keep coming back to the conviction that if you work hard at your act and build up your confidence in your talent you'll shine *whenever* you go on stage. Which means it's up to you to weigh up the pros and cons of the positions that suit you best.

For instance, it's true that nobody particularly enjoys going on first when the audience isn't properly warmed up yet (although a good talent-contest compère like Julie always makes a point of warming up the crowd before bringing on the first act).

Yet the very fact that most talent-contest audiences and judges know how hard it is to open a show means that if you can do well in this slot, you can often make an even better impression than if you go on when the show is in full swing. By going on first you also put paid to having to sit through the rest of the night racked with pre-show nerves as the rest of the performers will have to do.

Now for the cons: if the talent contest is being decided by an audience's or a judges' vote at the end, going on first may mean that at the end of the evening even the most dazzling opening number may have faded into distant memory.

In a professional show, going on last is the sign of the 'bill topper', the star of the show, and certainly if you can pull a dazzling performance out of the bag in this slot it will be very fresh in the voters' minds when it comes to decision time. But the inevitable delays and false starts that dog all but the most highly organised talent contests also mean that it can be very hard to keep focus and energy alive until the final curtain – something which applies not just to the performers but to the audience and judges too.

And the longer you wait to go on stage, the more chance of the ultimate horror: somebody else doing the song you were going to do. A professionally organised competition should have a system in place to prevent this occurrence, but we've seen it happen enough times to remind you to always have an alternative song up your sleeve (and the backing track or music for it, if necessary).

Whichever slot you choose to go on in and whatever song you sing, there is no 'special' trick to talent-contest performing – only the trick we're advocating throughout this whole book: treat every performance with the same level of enthusiasm, professionalism and polish whether it's one song at your friend's wedding or your own one-person show at the London Palladium.

To paraphrase Jesus again, 'Do the little things well and you have a lot more chance of being allowed have a go at the big stuff'. And once you've done your stuff, get off the stage and stop worrying about it.

In our own careers we've done great gigs which we didn't get a huge amount of praise for – after all the whole art of being professional is making it look 'easy'. Equally we've done gigs which the audience enjoyed, but which we felt we could have done better. The fact of the matter is that at whatever level of our careers we're at, if we're truly aiming for excellence the only person we're really in competition with is *us* at our personal best.

With that in mind, when judging time comes around don't focus so much on whether you've won or lost (although you wouldn't be human if you didn't hope you were the winner), but concentrate on what you've *learned* from this particular competition.

If you're not the winner, applaud politely no matter what your private opinion (may as well practise for when you come close second to Stevie Wonder at the Grammy Awards!), and ask yourself honestly what the winning act 'had' that you didn't have.

It almost certainly wasn't more talent – so was it more experience? More panache? A better choice of song? It might also be that they had more supporters in the audience or spent the interval chatting up the judges.

Take Whoopi Goldberg's advice and 'listen to what everyone has to say, whether you agree with it or not, because they might have something valuable to tell you, but when you've listened to all their advice, make sure to make your *own* mind up'.

This is particularly true if the judges or compère are giving 'feedback' on your act in front of the audience. Listen to what they have to say, especially if they are in some way connected with the music business or have some other professional expertise. As Whoopi says, they might have some useful advice for you. On the other hand, if they fancy themselves as cut-price *Pop Idol* judges and are simply making nasty comments and playing to the audience, don't let them get to you.

You may have to take comments from your own posse of supporters with a grain of salt too. On the one hand you'll find friends insisting that you were easily the best thing in the competition and that whole thing was rigged. But well-meaning as these comments may be, don't let them draw you into negativity and not learning from the whole experience.

Equally, you'll find the occasional well-meaning friend or parent who, genuinely wanting to spare you further disappointment, suggests that maybe you need to rethink this whole singing business and find another hobby. Again, thank them politely for their advice, but make your own mind up. (And if you make your mind up not to invite them to your next gig we certainly won't blame you.)

Don't assume either that because you didn't win a particular heat, you haven't impressed anyone. If there are any talent scouts at the contest, and particularly any good ones, they are there to spot potential, not necessarily just someone who is good at winning a particular type of competition. Have your business cards and any other marketing material (which we'll be telling you how to prepare in a later chapter) ready to hand out in case anyone expresses interest in seeing you again.

And then get busy practising for the next talent contest.

When all that practice finally pays off and *you're* the winner (and who's to say that won't happen sooner rather than later?), you may be asked to do an encore. Based on Julie's long experience of compèring such contests, her advice is don't worry about trying to 'top' yourself or show off, just sing the song you sang before, in the same way that won you your victory in the first place.

Enjoy your moment of glory . . . and then go home and start practising for your next talent contest.

Oh, and one final caution, which perhaps we should have put at the beginning of this section when you were still busy filling in your entry form: by all means enjoy any holiday, music centres or large wads of cash you win on the talent-contest circuit (and don't be shy about sending us large gifts care of our publishers!), but do read carefully the entry conditions of any talent contests you enter which include *recording* or *management contracts* as prizes.

The whole area of contracts and management deals is a minefield of which we'll talk later, and yes, it's perfectly possible that a credible record label or management company may choose the talent-contest route to recruit new acts. But *your* aim in signing any contract is to get the best deal for you as a performer, because you can be sure the company or person offering the contract will have set it up to protect *their* interests already. Make sure you're not signing away your right to negotiate your own deal by signing up to enter the contest.

Of course, if you're really determined to put yourself into the music marketplace there's no law that says you have to wait for your talent to be discovered on the contest circuit. You can start bringing yourself to the attention of people who are *already* looking for working singers by responding to audition calls in the music and theatrical trade press. So long as the ad doesn't specify Musician's Union or Equity members only (you'll find details of these important organisations in our resource section) you are perfectly at liberty to turn up and vie for work with all the other applicants.

It's a slightly different competition process to talent contests because there's no audience and the only prize is acceptance or rejection, but just as with talent contests, getting the basics right will greatly increase your chances of success.

Auditions

The main difference between talent contests and auditions is that, unless beginners have been specifically asked for, the people running the interview or audition are not doing it to support new talent, they are investing time and effort in finding a working singer who can do whatever job they need doing.

Does this mean beginners shouldn't apply? On the contrary, if you've got the confidence you can apply for anything. Just don't refer to the fact that you're a beginner and certainly don't expect any allowances for your lack of experience. This is the *business* end of show business and nobody has that kind of time.

Whatever type of audition you are doing, from a 'once off' pitch to an entertainments booker who is considering putting you on at their pub, club or even a whole chain of venues, to an audition for a more long-term position in a band or a musical, remember once again that the goal is not simply to demonstrate what a good singer you are, it is to demonstrate that you are the *right singer for the job.*

With that in mind, your first task is to find out as much as you can about the job on offer before you turn up. In some cases you may be given quite a lot of direction, from what kind of song to prepare to how to dress. In others you may have next to no information – which is a good reason to have a reasonably wide repertoire of material so you have a couple of song options up your sleeve when you get there.

Whatever you do before you get there, make sure you're clear as to the address you're heading for and what time your particular audition slot is, if you've been given one. Your 'show' starts as soon as you walk in the door, and if you're aiming to give the impression of being someone who's not just a good singer but a good *professional* singer, turning up late or flustered isn't going to help much.

Make sure you have the contact number of the person interviewing you in case unforeseen delays occur, but it has to be said at the outset that show business isn't the most understanding of worlds – miss your interview time and you could well find that your 'big break' has become somebody else's.

When you get to the audition you may have to wait in an outside room with other hopefuls. Don't let this throw you, even if all of them seem more beautiful, confident and sound better than you do.

Whatever your level of experience you need to go in with the attitude that you have as much chance of getting this job as anyone else. We know from our own experience – and have it on reliable authority from far bigger stars than us – that the singer who goes on before you will *always* sound better than you . . . in your own head. That's just the way nerves and self-confidence work.

It may well be that all the other candidates are just as nervous as you are, but are just hiding it better. Just as with dealing with nerves when facing a paying audience, remember that the interviewers *want* you to be successful. After all, they've gone to all the trouble of setting up this audition to find people they can work with.

The recent trend for *Pop Idol* type shows suggests that the standard interview set-up is three or more 'judges' sitting at a table, whom the singer has to perform in front of so they can make sarcastic comments. This may well be the case, given that life has a tendency to follow art, but it's just as likely you may find yourself auditioning to just one person or to a whole roomful of people setting up tables in a club, none of whom seem remotely interested in what you're doing.

If you're used to performing to larger audiences (or if you haven't performed at all except to an imaginary audience on the other side of your bedroom mirror) small set-ups like this can really throw you. The key thing is to decide that no matter what situation you find yourself in, you're going to focus on giving your best possible performance.

While you do need to direct your performance to the person or people interviewing you (it's not a great idea to demonstrate your stage presence by staring at your feet all though your set) it's important not to be influenced too much by how you perceive your show is going from the expressions on their faces.

In general, normal audience members will smile encouragingly and nod along in time to the music. The people you're auditioning for may do this, too, but it's more likely that they will watch you with blank expressions, talk to each other and write things down while you're in full flow. Don't be thrown by any of it, just keep on doing your best.

Contrary to what you see on television talent contests, it's unlikely that any nasty comments will be made about your performance. In fact you quite often won't get any immediate feedback at all, beyond the standard 'We'll let you know'.

If there are more people waiting to be seen behind you the best way to complete a good impression is to thank the interviewers politely and make a speedy exit. If they like you, you will hear from them . . . and in most circumstances if they don't like you, you won't hear from them ever again. So if there is silence after about a week you may as well start looking for other auditions. In fact, that's what you should be doing constantly anyway.

Of course, just as there are lots of different singers, there are lots of different kinds of interviewers too – for everything we've said above about the 'production line' type of audition, you may also come across the kind of interviewer who likes to chat. If you're all pumped up and focused on singing your big number, it can throw you when you suddenly get asked lots of questions about your previous experience, your musical tastes or occasionally about life, art and the universe.

Some of us are very confident in our singing, but a lot shyer when it comes to basic social interaction. If this is the case, you'll need to put a little practice into talking as well as speaking. Nobody's expecting you to be Noel Coward, but being able to hold a basic friendly conversation certainly helps reinforce that not only are you good on stage, but you'll be easy and pleasant to work with off stage too.

It's our experience that given a number of singers who are all at the same level musically and experience-wise, interviewers will choose the one who looks like they are most fun to work with every time.

Overall your attitude before, during and after singing should be pleasant and professional. Whether you are warm and friendly or a little cooler depends on you and the job you are going for – obviously if you are trying for a spot as a blues singer you may want to keep your natural chirpy charm a little more low key than usual. Equally, if you are auditioning for lead in a party band, an introspective, thoughtful personality may not be the best asset for the job.

Be careful, too, of taking an upfront attitude to extremes. Eagerness and enthusiasm about the audition will definitely go down well, but be wary of any suggestion of desperation creeping in: it's very unattractive. On the other hand, no matter how good your vocals and performance, try to avoid appearing either arrogant or so laid back about the whole thing that you don't care about the project at all.

Show business is all about ego, and the egos of producers, music directors and venue managers can be just as sensitive as those of performers. Having said that, there's no need to be a complete doormat either.

In particular, you may find that that nerves lead even the most prepared performer to start off on the wrong note, or forget the words to the song. Apologise quickly, start over and do your best. If you forget the words you may even win some brownie points by 'winging it' and allowing your natural personality to shine through.

Just avoid long drawn out and profuse 'sorrys'. The art of performance is not about drawing attention to problems and mistakes, it is about coping with them.

In dressing for an audition or interview, it's perfectly acceptable to 'glam up' a little bit – after all you are aiming for stardom. But unless it's a fundamental part of your own particular stage image, don't overdress, and in particular don't wear an outfit you're uncomfortable with or not used to performing in just for the audition – it will be just one more thing to worry about and a further distraction from doing your best.

Note to female performers: avoid wearing exceptionally low-cut tops. If you're not used to doing so your breasts (and the danger of them popping out) will distract you more than your audience. If it's the interviewers you're trying to distract, forget it – this is one industry in which most people really have 'seen it all'. Just to even the score we'd also caution male performers about turning up in tight leather trousers. Yes, Ricky Martin or

Brian Ferry may get away with them, but they usually won't be asked to try a dance routine during the audition, and if they are, can afford to buy a new pair of pants to replace split ones.

Depending on the kind of singing job you are going for, have at least a couple of different songs prepared. Ideally these should be songs that show your voice off to best advantage, and it helps if it's a song that the interviewer (and any musicians lined up to accompany you) vaguely know, although it's probably best to avoid the hit song of the moment, as the chances are several other interviewees will have decided it's the perfect song for them too.

Listen very carefully to any information you get about the audition beforehand. Many singers auditioning for pop bands ruin their chances by only knowing songs which are 'R & B' and vice versa. Yes, a good voice is a good voice and anyone with a decent musical ear should be able to discern that a good R & B singer can also sing pop, but it's not the interviewer's job to discern anything – it's *your* job to pick the right song in the first place.

If you have favourite audition songs, it's a good idea to have both the backing track and the sheet music available so you can sing them. You don't want to find you can't do your show-stopping number because the pianist doesn't know the notes. Equally, if you're used to singing the song to your own backing track, you need to be flexible enough to be able to do it with a live musician too, who may not hit the notes in exactly the same places. Make sure you can sing the song well a cappella in case there's a complete breakdown of technology.

Another reason for having a few extra songs you are really comfortable with is quite simply that musical tastes are very subjective. 'I *hate* that song' doesn't really inspire confidence in you when the interviewer tells you so just before you're about to sing it.

Should you just sing the song or 'perform' it? We would go for putting on a performance every time, even if it's to an audience of one and you feel slightly embarrassed.

People in the music business often affect a cynical/laid-back attitude which they fondly imagine is 'cool'. Most of the time it's just irritating, but if they are the ones calling the tune you'll have to accept them for what they are. What you need to avoid doing is getting drawn into bringing the same attitude to your own performance. There's nothing cool about not giving it your best shot, and there is much more chance of blowing an audition through not showing enough enthusiasm than showing too much of it.

While many auditions operate on the 'conveyor belt' principle of in and out in a couple of minutes, you may be asked questions about your previous experience, current plans and future goals.

In terms of your previous experience it's always a good policy to be honest about it, not just from a moral point of view, but because show business can be a very small world. Don't tell them you sang in a particular club or backed a particular performer if you didn't. Murphy's Law will usually guarantee that someone on the interview panel has a friend who manages the same club or is going out with the same singer.

More to the point, people will see *exactly* how much performance experience you really have when you open your mouth to sing. It's always a good idea to surprise your audience by exceeding their expectations rather than giving the impression that you're Elvis, Madonna and Pavarotti rolled into one and setting yourself up for a fall.

When it comes to your current plans be equally honest, particularly if it's a long-term job. If you are currently working in a day job, say so, making it clear that if you get chosen for this gig, you'll make whatever time is needed available. The 'small world' principle applies here, too – you can have by far the best voice and most exciting stage persona around but if you keep turning up for auditions, getting offers and then telling people that sorry, you can only work on your nights off from the chip shop, word will start to spread among annoyed producers and bookers.

Being honest, though, doesn't mean you necessarily have to reveal all about any other music projects you are working on at the same time, particularly if you are working on them with other people. For instance, if you are working with a producer doing vocals for some dance tracks, it's fine to let people know about it as it establishes that you are a working singer and in demand, but you don't have to go into great detail on what the tracks sound like, or which label they are targeted at, even if pumped for more information. Besides breaching confidence there's a basic principle that interviewers in every business bear in mind: if this person is spilling someone else's trade secrets all over the place, who will they be spilling *my* secrets to if they become part of this operation?

It goes without saying that you should *never* badmouth anyone else in the business during an interview regardless of your previous experiences, even if the interviewers themselves are badmouthing them. Bitching, gossip and paranoia are part and parcel of show business, but so is the principle of 'what goes around comes around'.

If asked about your goals and ambitions, again be honest but use wisdom. If you're auditioning for a group, it's probably best to play down the elements of your game plan that scream 'I want a solo career'.

For group auditions, existing or under construction, you may be asked to harmonise with other singers. Remember that what you're trying to demonstrate is that you are a team player: sing as well as you can, but don't try to out-sing other people. For all you know the group may already have a 'leader', and out-singing that person will only lead you to the exit door.

Usually you'll be told if dance skills are a requirement for the audition. If they are, make sure you've done a little practice beforehand – singing and dancing at the same time can leave you breathless if you're not used to it. So can leaping around in heavy boots, so make sure you're wearing something more suitable.

And don't worry if you're not Fred Astaire – there may be a choreographer on hand to run you through a few steps individually or with other hopefuls. Watch carefully what you're being asked to do, and then give it your best shot. Usually what choreographers are looking for is enthusiasm, a basic memory for steps, however slow, and a willingness to learn.

As with talent contests, whether or not you get through a particular audition is a very subjective matter. It's not unknown for a singer to be turned down as unsuitable for one job, but be remembered by the producer or casting director and called back for another part or perhaps even another job.

And anyhow you should be far too busy applying for other auditions to sit waiting by the phone, not to mention busy working on marketing yourself and generating your own work. Not sure how to do that? Good, because it's this second aspect of job finding that we're looking at in our next chapter.

Chapter Five

Start Spreadin' the News

Marketing for the working singer

A few years ago John was organising a celebrity event with Dionne, the entertainments editor of a national newspaper. In one meeting at the newspaper office Dionne was suddenly summoned to the reception area. A young musician had turned up, insisting on playing a copy of his latest release and refusing to leave until he spoke to Dionne in person.

Marketing tip number one: normally, if you turn up at a newspaper office unannounced and make demands like that, the only person you're likely to have a 'one to one' with is a hefty member of the security staff. But it was lunchtime and the relief receptionist wasn't used to such high-pressure hassle, so she'd given in and called Dionne downstairs.

Being a kind-hearted soul, and rather impressed by the young man's passion and commitment, the journalist patiently explained that dragging already busy people out of meetings was *not* the best way to warm them up for listening to a demo, no matter how promising. However *if* he was prepared to wait until the meeting was finished, and *if* she had a spare moment before her next meeting, Dionne promised she'd come back and see him then.

So she went back to the meeting about the show, and, as with all planning meetings, it went way over time. But Dionne went back out to chat to the young singer anyhow. Unfortunately in the interim period frustration and impatience had led him to smash up the reception desk.

You'll be unsurprised to hear that his record was not promoted in that particular paper.

There are a couple of interesting lessons from that story. Number one is, as every experienced singer and musician knows, that you can have the greatest sound and stage show in the world and it won't do you any good if you can't bring it to everyone else's attention.

Number two, the only one who really believes strongly enough in your ability to sell you to the rest of the world is you. And number three, because the rest of the world has its own life to lead and many other artists vying for its attention, making yourself stand out is a 'long haul' process.

There's sometimes a very fine line between 'nuisance' and the 'next big thing'.

Although like that young musician, it's quite easy to get bitter and frustrated (or simply to give up), neither one of those approaches ever got anyone to the top. Look at any 'overnight success' and there's usually been a long journey behind the scenes to get there. In fact if there hasn't been that long journey, many overnight successes are so unprepared that it really is all over the following morning.

So if you're ready to make the long journey, the key to successful marketing is to make the most of all the contacts you make along the way

Your mailing list

Open any CD case, log onto your favourite singer's website or attend any sell-out concert and the chances are you'll be asked for your name or address. Yes, you may also be asked some questions about your preferences in music, films and other things, you may be asked some details about your occupation, background and income, you may even get a free T-shirt thrown in.

But most of all what the people behind the CDs, websites and concerts want is your precious name and address, so they can lead you to more CDs, websites and concerts you'll be interested in spending your hard-earned cash on. The beauty of this system is that, unlike double glazing, motor insurance or multilevel marketing schemes, which have to convince customers they are useful, most people who are fans of a particular singer or style of music are more than happy to be kept up to date with more opportunities to spend money on things they like.

Even if you're working out of your bedsit rather than the plush offices of an international record company, you can take a leaf out of their book and start compiling your mailing list today. It's probably your most important marketing tool of all – in fact if you work hard enough at it, it could be one of the major factors in speeding your move from bedsit to that plush office.

Strictly speaking, you need a master list that you can sort into two mailing lists. The first one is your fan base, the name, address and contact details for everyone who's ever come to your gigs, sent you a fan letter or expressed interest in any aspect of your work. Make it a habit that you never let one of these people get away without getting contact details for them. You can have mailing-list forms at your gigs (you need to have your own, as if the venue has one they'll hang on to it for dear life). You can have a simple 'pop up' form on your website. Or if someone comes up after a gig to tell you they enjoyed what you did, you can simply ask for their name and address 'so I can let you know about my next gig/my new CD/send you a free T-shirt'.

The basic principle is why should you bust a gut 'cold-selling' each new gig or project to the attention of new people when you have an existing group of people who are already pre-sold on your work?

Mailing list number two is all the people in the industry who can give you the chance to make new fans. You can't perform for an audience unless you have a venue to perform in, so you need to be selling yourself to the entertainment bookers of whatever venue you've set your sights on. You can't let people know how great the gig was unless someone is there to review it, so you need to attract the journalists whose opinion people respect. And if you want someone to come and record the gig, then radio producers and A & R people need to be in your sights. (That's two more sub-lists to compile.)

All the lists are related: venues need to put bums on seats, journalists need to bump up circulation figures, record companies need to know there's an audience for their product.

If you can prove you've got a big enough fan base you're a long way along the road to getting these people to take you seriously.

Market research

Whenever we ask an aspiring singer who they want their music to appeal to, the usual answer is 'everybody'. It's certainly true that the best entertainers can appeal to every sort of audience regardless of age, sex or musical preference, but when you've got a limited marketing budget and an even more limited 'marketing team' (possibly just you in your spare time) 'everybody' is a pretty big market to be aiming for.

Just as you'll find it invaluable to really crystallise what your vision is for your singing career, try to work out exactly who your primary audience is. These are the people who are likely to pick up on your sound and provide the biggest fan base in the shortest space of time.

Sometimes there can be a particular audience that you really want to reach – for many singers it's their own peer-group audience, be they teenagers or thirty-somethings. Other entertainers go for a different market, which though smaller, can often be easier to conquer – one singer we know who enjoyed singing classics and jazz standards discovered a lucrative market putting on afternoon shows for old age pensioners. (Lucrative because many councils and social services organisations have funding available for the entertainment of pensioners.)

Whoever you decide is your typical audience, you then need to think about their likes and dislikes. Where do they go for entertainment? What TV and radio shows do they watch? Which record labels do their favourite artists record on?

You need to start visiting those venues, watching those shows and listening to those recordings, but not just for entertainment purposes. Try really hard to identify common elements in delivery, packaging or subject matter which make these particular performers or productions appeal to the target audience. Congratulations – you're now doing market research.

The next step is to attract the attention of the appropriate people to bring you in front of your chosen market. Is it the A & R person for a specific label? Is it the producer of a certain show or an influential journalist that everybody in that area of the business reads? These are your mailing list people – but you can't put them on the list until you find out who they are.

Contacts

The reason beginning singers (and many more experienced ones) usually give us for not being able to reach that elusive audience of 'everybody' is that they 'just don't have the contacts'.

It's true that if you could just pick up the phone and call the right people things might move a lot quicker, but even if you're not on first-name terms with them (their loss!) right now, you can certainly improve your chances of getting your name in front of the right people by putting some research time into finding out who the right people actually are.

Keep an eye on the music trade press, search on the Internet, pick up the phone, dial the company switchboard and ask. Whether it's the chief buyer of your local record store or the head of senior citizens' recreation at your local council, once you've got a specific name and title you have some one to direct your marketing to.

And now that you've got that name, let's look at some of the things you may want to send them.

Marketing materials

Elsewhere in this book we've stressed the overall importance of your image as a singer. Your marketing and business communications are an important part of this image – in fact as they are quite often the *first* contact someone will have with you, this is one of the most vital areas to get right.

Particularly at the beginning of your career you may not have a huge (or even any) marketing budget, but at least try to make the best of what you do have through neatness, professionalism and attention to detail.

If your budget stretches to having your own letterhead, wonderful. It's even better if you can persuade a design-minded friend to come up with a 'logo' for you. But at the very least make sure every piece of print that has your name on it is clean, clear and on good quality paper. It's hardly going to persuade anyone that you are a stylish, experienced act if the letter telling them so is crumpled, handwritten and accompanied by a grainy second-generation copy of a photo that looks like it would be more at home on the inside of a phone box.

(The same applies, by the way, even if you are a tattooed wildman rocker – the hairier the megastar the more likely they can afford to hire a team of 'suits' to do all the marketing and PR work. Until you can afford a similar team you're going to have to play both roles yourself.)

Whether or not you can afford to get a professional letterhead designed we would certainly encourage you to get that most un-rock 'n' roll of accessories, a decent set of business cards, as soon as you start out. Business cards are small enough to carry with you when you are gigging, so that when someone approaches you after a show to (hopefully) offer you more work you can give them your contact details easily instead of scrabbling round with biros and backs of cigarette packets.

Also, cards are great to have on hand when unexpected marketing opportunities arise: you never know who you may come in contact with in the course of your day job or at a social occasion who may have need of a singer or contacts in the music or entertainment industry.

When you do hand them your card, try to make sure it's not one of the mass-produced ones that you get from vending machines – if *you're* an original the information you give to people should be too.

Right from the start, try to make your letters, biographies and any other piece of communication as polished and error-free as possible. This means checking spellings, grammar, and unless you're sending a thank-you card or short personal note, making sure everything is typed rather than handwritten. Whether you're pitching a club owner to get on stage at their venue or a record producer to listen to your tracks, they'll certainly be wondering how good your voice and performance skills are . . . but they'll also be influenced by more mundane concerns such as how professional you are, will you turn up on time, is it worth their giving valuable time to finding out more about you? If you can't even be bothered to make your initial communication look professional it doesn't exactly give the impression that your attitude to your music will be any different.

If writing or typing isn't your strong suit get someone else to help you out. As your career progresses you'll find you use the same letters and documents over and over again, from confirming gig bookings to sending out invoices, so it will save a lot of time to have your standard letters saved on a computer disk so you can customise them and send them out at as needed.

While it's no surprise to us that not every performer is as comfortable with administration as they are with entertaining – and isn't it lucky for agents and managers and personal assistants that they aren't? – we never thought we'd have to offer advice on how to put a piece of paper into an envelope. Sadly, we have frequently been on the receiving end of letters and packages which a singer has obviously spent a lot of time composing and printing on decent paper, and then crammed into an envelope which is too small or too flimsy to survive in the post.

Test marketing

A very good way to gauge how effective your sales and marketing is, is to identify someone who works in business – music or show business preferably, but any business will do – and send them your promotional package as if they have never heard of you. Ask them to tell you honestly what impression of you they would form from the package alone and if it would prompt them to pick up the phone and find out more about you. If you can manage enough detachment you could even try sending a sample package to yourself. Just as every performer can learn a lot from 'sitting in their own audience', putting yourself in the place of the recipient of your promotional material can identify some easily made but nonetheless fundamental oversights.

Recently John acted as a 'pretend music executive' for a friend. The package which arrived was very well presented, in a good sturdy envelope with an impressive CD and bubbly and catchy letter. If he had been a real prospective employer he would definitely have contacted the artist to find out more. Unfortunately, nowhere in the package had the performer remembered to include a contact number.

Sadly, stories of talent scouts scouring the country for unknown but brilliant performers mostly belong to the movies. Make a basic (and quite common) error like forgetting to include contact details and your big break is likely to go to an equally talented singer who pays more attention to detail.

So assuming your letter does arrive in one piece and you've remembered to include your contact details, what can you do to help ensure that the recipient is encouraged to use them and get back to you?

Getting the person's name right helps. From the landlord of your local pub to the head of Sony records, a letter is far more likely to be dealt with if it is addressed to a specific person rather than just a job title. Yes, we know you wouldn't send your demo tape addressed to 'Head of Sony Records' and expect to get an answer, but even in a small venue 'The Landlord' may not be the right person to send it to either – there may be another staff member or maybe even an outside booker who handles the music details.

Unless you've been given a personal contact for someone you're writing to it's well worth a phone call to find out exactly who to send your stuff to . . . and even if you have been given a contact, it's worth a call to check how their name is spelt. People are very sensitive about their names and titles at the best of times, and particularly so in the ego-driven world of show business, so there's no surer way to annoy someone in a letter than by getting their name wrong.

Whatever the title or position of the person you're writing to, write on the assumption that they are both important and busy. Yes, you're a singer not an insurance broker so you don't have to be ultra-formal ('Dear Sir, I have pleasure in sending you my demo tape for consideration' doesn't sound quite right if you're a thrash metal musician), but equally letters which are too jokey or tell your entire life story are liable to irritate more than attract.

Basically, your initial approach should tell the reader who you are, tell them what's unique or different about you, tell them what you've got to offer them specifically, tell them what you've enclosed to demonstrate you can deliver (i.e. CDs, photos, videos or bio), and finally tell them what they need to do or who they need to contact to find out more.

Market research is when you find out what a venue or a company is looking for and tell them how you are the solution to their search. More to the point, market research stops you wasting time and money pitching to wrong targets – one of the reasons why the majority of pitches are dead in the water before the envelope is even opened.

It's pretty pointless selling yourself as a jazz singer to a pub which only puts on folk or country and western acts, or as an R & B singer to a label that only releases indie pop, yet many singers we know have wasted time and energy doing just this, when a simple phone call would have saved disappointment. Equally, if you're an up-and-coming soul diva, the label which has just signed an up-and-coming soul diva may not be the best one to send your demo to, although a label which is in direct competition might be.

And yes, if you're talented and determined enough you *can* get a venue or label to change its music policy to make room for you – but you still need to know what that music policy is in the first place.

Given that the music industry is full of PR companies and marketing specialists working night and day to come up with stunts and schemes to make their artists stand out from the crowd, can you employ the same techniques to get your stuff noticed? Well of course you can, depending on the style of music you're into. The story of a rock band who sent a home-made video to various A & R people with a lollypop Sellotaped to the case and a card saying 'Suck it and See' springs to mind. Just remember that however you pitch your work, your main effort and expense needs to go into producing performances and demos that deliver on your promises. You don't want to get a response back saying 'I've seen it. It sucks.'

Flash bang wallop

A well-known performer was interviewed about his early days trekking around the country playing every venue no matter how tatty, small or cheap. In particular he recalled a venue which was so small it only had one power point, so he was given the choice of performing either with sound or with lights. 'I chose lights', he said. Good choice.

For better or for worse music is becoming as much about the visual as it is about sound, and this is particularly true when you are promoting yourself. We have already discussed image elsewhere in the book, and you'll know that we are strongly of the opinion that as long as you have talent and determination and are prepared to play to your strengths, you can make a good stab at being a working singer no matter what size, shape, age or race you are. But however you look, for most people the first point of contact with your look will not be through your live show or your music, but through your photo.

With this in mind, it's worth getting your photos done as soon as you can, but also worth putting time and effort into getting them right. Because photos are such a powerful marketing tool you're going to go through a lot of them, but photo shoots are expensive so it's well worth getting something good that you can go on using for some time.

Please, please, please, if at all possible, get your photographs taken by a professional photographer, and preferably one who is used to taking shots of performers. It doesn't matter how good a photographer your best friend is, or how hi-tech your camera. 'Home-made' photos instantly mark you out as an amateur – and we've also been sent enough passport photos, graduation photos and masterpieces by the local wedding photographer to assure you that the impression they create is, if possible, even worse.

The best way to get proper photos done is to get another performer you know who has good photos to put you in contact with the person who took them. If you don't know anyone, trade papers like *The Stage* have small ads from many specialist photographers plying for trade. (Note for females: make sure you don't confuse the ads for portrait photographers with the ads for photographers seeking 'glamour models'.)

Whether or not you have been recommended to a particular photographer, ask to see examples of their work. Just like singers, each photographer has their own individual style, and it's worth shopping around to find one that suits you. Bear in mind that it is not the photographer's job to create your 'image' for you – that's something you should have worked out in advance. What you are looking for is someone who can capture that image and show it off to best advantage.

It goes without saying that a good photographer should put you at your ease, and listen to your ideas, even if they have better ideas based on their own experience. On the other hand, if the photographer doesn't seem particularly bothered or interested in what you want to achieve you are probably better off looking elsewhere.

It's usually a good idea to check out a couple of photographers price-wise before making a final decision. More expensive doesn't necessarily mean better. Equally, someone who is very much cheaper than the average should ring alarm bells in terms of quality.

However much you are paying, make sure you are very clear on what you are getting for your money. Many photographers charge for the initial photo session, out of which you will get a contact sheet of all the shots taken and then prints of the photos you choose. Although many photographers will keep your negatives on file digitally so they can print up more copies if you need them, it's usually more economical to have your chosen shot printed up and then have it mass produced by one of the many 'repro' houses which advertise in the trade magazines.

In bygone times, good-quality black and white photos were the best ones for the cash-strapped beginner to choose, for economic reasons. These days black and white film costs as much if not more than colour, but monochrome photos are still the most versatile: they can be reproduced in all kinds of media and, taken properly, can look 'classy' in a way that suits many singers' images. By all means get good colour shots too – but even when you've got them, make sure they also look well when reproduced in black and white, as they might be in a newspaper article or on a flyer.

In general, the more photos you order the less the cost of each one, so – assuming you've got a good-quality photo to start with – get as many as you can printed so you've got a good supply available. While the classic 8″ × 10″ shots are very nice, postcard-size is a lot more versatile and economic if the paying work hasn't started rolling in just yet.

How does one achieve photos that might lead to paying work? A little preparation before the photo session helps. For a start, try to book the session for a time when you can get there easily and in good form – as already mentioned in the context of getting to auditions on time, arriving late and sweaty from a crowded bus won't help to create a glamorous image.

Unlike an actor who may want a photograph which portrays them as a 'blank canvas' on which a casting director can project whatever character they are looking for (sorry if we've just offended any actors reading this), a singer's photo should look reasonably close to the image they present on stage.

So allow time to change into your stage gear or something in line with the same image, and also to 'get into character' if, as is often the case, your stage persona is raunchier, rockier or more exaggerated than your everyday self.

It may or may not help the photographer to have a tape or a visual image of you in performance, but even if it just helps you, have that sort of stuff on hand if you need it. Remember that ultimately you are the only one who knows what image you want to put across and it's worth focusing until you get it.

Actors are often advised to wear little if any make-up for their photos, to allow their 'natural' selves to shine through. Again, slightly different advice may be needed for a singer, particularly if your stage persona is glamorous or sophisticated. A good photographer should be able to adjust the lighting to the best effect even if you are just wearing normal make-up, but if you have make-up people or stylists as part of your support team it's a good idea to get them involved or at least to get their advice before the session, always bearing in mind that professional advice and experience should be what you are after, not interference from well-meaning friends.

Should you go for a 'head and shoulders' shot as most actors do or a 'full body' picture? That really depends on you and your act: for instance, if you play a guitar or some other instrument it makes sense to include it in your picture (but please, no Chuck Berry-style 'duck walking' unless you are a revival or comedy act). If 'sexy' is a factor in your image, again a full-body shot would make sense (remembering that the difference between 'sexy' and 'tacky' in both dress and pose can usually be summed up as 'trying too hard').

On the other hand you might want to take a lead from Julie's own photo (see page opposite), which is simple but showcases the bubbly personality which keeps her in demand as a compère and radio personality as well as a singer.

It is of course Murphy's Law that on the day of your photo session something will happen to depress you, distract you and generally make you feel like hiding your head under the bedcovers rather than showing your talents off to the world. It's

also the nature particularly of female performers (but also more male performers than may care to admit it) that we are never 100 per cent happy with our physical appearance – and the prospect of being photographed is especially likely to bring all those insecurities to the fore.

However you feel on the day, treat the photo session just like you would a show, and make the camera your audience. Since you are looking for a shot that will be usable for a year or two, try to visualise where you hope to be in a year or two, and step into that image right now. Today you may have to walk home from the session because you can't afford the bus fare, but your dream is to open in a quality venue with your own sell-out show . . . so for the purpose of the photo session start acting out that dream as if it's already happening.

The first thing the booker at a quality venue is going to look for before booking a performer for a show, is someone who looks like they can sell out a show, and if you *don't* believe it how can you make the rest of us do so?

It's not just for our benefit either if you can make yourself believe that you are a real star, and give off that image if only for the duration of the photo shoot, that same photo can act as a powerful inspiration during the inevitable times when the business feels like all hard slog and your dreams seem far away.

Demo tapes and CDs

While a photo is one of your most important selling devices, some audio evidence that you actually can sing is obviously a pretty useful marketing tool for a singer to have, too.

Demo tapes and CDs are not much different from photographs in that there are a lot of companies offering both recording and reproduction services (once again look for ads in the trade press or better still, for personal recommendations).

Unlike photos, however, advances in home recording techniques and developments in PC technology such as CD burning mean that it might just be possible to get a good-quality result without breaking the bank.

'Quality' is still the watchword, however. Increasingly, the standard for song demos is production which sounds so professional that the demo sounds almost indistinguishable from songs already in the charts. While the demos we're talking about here are just to give an example of what you sound like in action, it's still true that any cheap, shoddy production or poorly recorded sound will make you sound amateur and do you more harm than good.

If you're prepared to negotiate and record at strange hours of the day or night, you may find that recording studios do cheaper rates in 'off times'. Many studios offer package deals where you get the studio time plus an engineer thrown in. Remember, however, that just like a photographer, there are some recording engineers who can be very knowledgeable and can help you get the best out of your studio time, but they are *not* the same thing as a producer. There are also some real 'cowboys'. Before going into the studio you must have a good idea of the sound you want to achieve and the aspects of your voice and personality you want the demo to 'sell'. Booking a little more studio time than you think you need is a good idea if you can at all afford it: you may want to do a couple of 'takes' to get your sound right, and if you're working against the clock, pressure and stress and the necessity of settling for 'good' rather than 'great' may creep into your vocal.

Once again the principle of assuming that the people listening to your demo are going to be busy is a good one to apply. A couple of tracks showing your versatility – say a ballad and a more high-energy number – can be much stronger than a whole slew of tracks which essentially sound the same. The main purpose of any demo/promotional package is to get the recipient to make further contact with you, and an 'I want to hear more' reaction is much more useful than 'when is this tape ever going to end?'

Actually, the end is likely to come very quickly: most music professionals can tell after the first 30 seconds whether a singer 'grabs' them and sadly, if you don't, they are unlikely to waste time listening to the rest of the track.

With this in mind, try to exercise the same creativity when you put together your demo as you do when you work on your live set. Make sure your demo reflects the personality and image you are trying to convey in the rest of your package. If, for instance, you are pitching yourself to a venue manager as an exciting all-round entertainer who can really whip a party audience into a frenzy, a demo tape consisting of gentle and heartfelt ballads is only going to work against getting you the gig, no matter how well you sing them. Equally, you can have an amazing voice, the effect of which can be completely destroyed when the engineer puts it on top of an horrendous 'last year' backing track. Choose your studio wisely. (Check out www.makehits.com for much more on this subject.)

When you get your CD or tapes reproduced think about how best to present them – remember that when they come out of the package (hopefully a padded one so they arrive in good condition) the first impact they make on the recipient is visual.

Some artists go all out and have professionally designed inlay cards and gatefold sleeves for their demo material. If your budget or creativity doesn't stretch quite this far, at least make sure you have your contact details neatly on the CD or tape. Discs and cassettes can easily become separated from the rest of your package.

Incidentally, if you do label your CDs by hand make sure you put the label on properly – a prospective client is not going to warm to your vocals if the label comes off your CD and they have to spend half an hour trying to remove the remains of it from their expensive sound system.

Videos/CD-ROMs

If you have good-quality video clips of your performance it can certainly help your marketing package to include them on cassette or CD-ROM. But everything we have said about photos and demo tapes applies here in spades, in particular the bits relating to quality. You may be one of the world's most exciting entertainers, able to hold an audience in the palm of your hand, but a home-made video, shot in bad light from the third row of your cousin's wedding reception, is hardly likely to confirm your reputation. (Please don't think we're exaggerating here – the quality of much of the video we get sent, often from experienced performers who should know better, would honestly make you weep.)

A look at the credits of any professional concert video, with multiple cameras and extensive post-production and sound remixing, will confirm just how much the professionals spend on getting things right. And even then what is sold as a 'live concert performance' is quite frequently several live concert performances shot on different nights with the best bits edited together to give the illusion of the perfect show.

You may not be able to stump up a multi-million-dollar production budget just yet, but if you are planning to use video as part of your selling package you must be prepared to invest a reasonable amount of money in proper equipment and people who know how to operate it. And you also need to be able to communicate to the video team what you are trying to achieve before you go on stage – you can't be worrying about how the video's going to turn out when you're in the spotlight trying to give a show that's worth capturing on tape.

Reviews and showreels

No matter how impressive your photos, demos and other promotional material, people in the music business, as elsewhere, often have a touching reluctance to set as much store by the evidence of their own eyes and instincts as by the confirmation of somebody else. Many medical products are sold on the back of recommendations from 'real life doctors', pet foods are promoted as the ones that 'nine out of ten owners prefer', and a good press review even if it's just one line long is likely to appear on an artist's promos and posters for many years.

'A stunning performer', 'Stylish, sexy, sensational', 'The next big thing': if anyone has said something complimentary about you in print, hang on to it and let other people know about it.

It's human nature that before we invest our time or hard-earned cash in something, we like to know that someone else has been there before us. One or two good reviews from respected sources can make all the difference in persuading someone to book us, record us or spend money on a ticket to come and see us.

And yes, we know that there are people who brazenly make up press quotes and sometimes entire reviews. All we can say is that's a moral issue between you and your conscience (and remind you that whatever claims you make for your act in your promotional material should be things you can actually deliver on when the curtain goes up).

As for the even more common practice of taking just the best bits of reviews, often out of context, well let's just say that if your posters and flyers say 'Amazing! – *The Times*' while the original *Times* reviewer said 'It's amazing that anyone this bad should actually be on stage' it might be best if you put your promotional work aside and put in a lot more rehearsal before anyone actually comes to see you.

On a more serious note, if you do get good reviews whether as an individual or for shows you have been in, make sure you get several copies of them to keep (you can usually buy back numbers from the publication if you miss the news-stand edition). A good clippings selection – neatly and properly photocopied, of course – can look very impressive when included in your package.

By the way, you don't have to just wait and hope the press will turn up to see you do your stuff. As long as you are confident that you can deliver the goods, why not take the bull by the horns and invite music critics and reviewers to your upcoming gigs?

Yes, music writers, particularly the influential ones, get invited to many more events than they can actually get to, but anyone who works in the press will tell you that journalists also have deadlines and empty spaces to fill on a regular basis, and it might just be that your letter or press release arrives at a time when they are stuck for inspiration. The better you get at identifying what's unique and exciting about your act, the more chance you will have of convincing the press that you are worth coming down to see.

If you're appearing in professional shows or doing special charity gigs it may be that the venue or organisers are already doing publicity, but most of us find that the only way of guaranteeing the best possible coverage is taking responsibility for doing it ourselves and viewing whatever marketing anyone else does as a bonus.

Just as with letters and other elements of your promotion, make sure that you have your contact numbers on any press information you send out, as well as details of the date and time of the gig.

Although major journalists don't usually worry about admission fees, a line like 'Please contact me if you would like to come along and I will arrange to put you on the guest list' may attract the attention of writers for smaller publications. (Check in advance that you can do this, of course.)

If you're aiming to build up a reputation in your local area, don't underestimate the power of the local press. But also don't underestimate the tendency of journalists to phone up, express interest in coming and then not show up on the night. Don't take it personally – just build on that initial spark of interest and contact them again about your next gig. When it comes to marketing yourself, perseverance is often as important as one big splash.

Another scenario, of course, is that the journalist does show up, has a good time and then writes nothing about you or your gig. It's not unknown for members of the press to use their 'power' to 'blag' and 'lig' their way through life, but most times the journalist probably did write the piece but it got bounced because of lack of space. Again, keep them on your press list and continue sending them information.

(Of course, just because you were the one who invited the journalist to the gig doesn't mean they won't write a bad review of your act . . . or write a glowing review of somebody else on the bill who takes their fancy. Resist all temptation to complain, and rise above it – although when you win your Grammy award you may want to leave that particular person off the guest list.)

You can also actively pitch yourself to television shows, instead of sitting around waiting for them to come and discover you. As with local papers, you probably have more chance of getting onto local TV and smaller stations through the direct approach. Although there are a lot of 'Pop Stars' and 'Reality' shows on TV at the time of writing, they usually have a pre-established audition process. In fact the audition process is quite often part of the show itself.

Such opportunities are usually promoted quite heavily in the popular media, but if you want to get a 'head start' on approaching music and entertainment shows, keep an eye on the broadcasting trade press, which reports on programmes which are being commissioned six months or even a year in advance and will usually tell you which production company is making which show.

When it comes to existing or long-running shows you can find all the production details and relevant names on the end credits. Forward-thinking performers keep notes of names which keep popping up in the credits of music and light entertainment shows and include them on their mailing lists.

If you do get TV work, whether on local, cable or national TV, you may want to put together a showreel from the best bits to help you get more work later on. If possible, ask the TV company for a tape, as a copy recorded off your mum's telly won't have the same sharpness, particularly if it has to be recopied so you can make more videos to send out. It's worth investing in some editing to put the highlights of your TV work on one tape, and even if you only have one TV appearance under your belt, to edit down so that's the only thing on the tape. It doesn't really create the best impression if your client has to fast forward through two hours of breakfast TV including adverts to get to your two minutes of fame.

Website

Your own website can be a highly effective marketing tool and a great way of building up your fan base – you can have photos, biographical information, music downloads, you can even sell CDs, T-shirts and other merchandise if you have a real business head. These days there are enough simple software packages around that even if you're the least 'techie' singer you can design and construct an all-singing, all-dancing site that reflects your own unique image and personality with relative ease (relative ease meaning you'll probably have to ask a teenage relative to help you). But the one key thing you need to remember about websites is that the most amazing site in the world is no good if nobody actually logs onto it.

Once you've got a web address (search to see if you can register your stage name or a variation of it) you will need to publicise it as much as possible, and that often involves going back to old-fashioned letter, poster and print methods.

Conclusion

As we said at the beginning, the only person who can really market you effectively is you: spend time practising some or all of the above marketing methods and you'll learn not just more about marketing, but a lot more about your fan base and the elements of your act that appeal to them. When you have generated enough interest through your own efforts to the point where some other person or company is interested in coming on board and marketing you, having done the job yourself will ensure that when your career starts 'going places' it goes to the places you had in mind in your original vision.

Speaking of that vision, we've stressed the need for precision and care in looking after your marketing. Something that many singers forget is that the same care needs to be taken in looking after themselves. In the next chapter we'll try to make sure that not only do you go places, but that you get there in one piece.

Chapter Six

I've Got You Under My Skin

Protecting your greatest asset – your health

In an industry notorious for sex, drugs and rock 'n' roll, any chapter on taking care of your voice, physique and mental health is in danger of sounding preachy. On the other hand, we know a lot of singers, famous and infamous, who as they get older wish they'd spent a bit less time on the sex and drugs and a bit more on the rock 'n' roll. And those are just the lucky ones – the history of music includes a long, long rollcall of singers who have ended up bankrupt, suicidal or dead.

On a less dramatic note, the simple fact is that if you take care of yourself better, you perform better, and if you want confirmation of that take a look at the guitar players, drummers and keyboard players you work alongside. Not as role models of good heath and clean living in themselves, you understand – when it comes to hotel wrecking and high living, musicians as a species could give the citizens of Soddom a run for their money. However, accidentally knock over somebody's drum kit or tread on a guitar and you'll soon learn that serious musos treat their instruments with far more respect than they treat their own bodies. From expensive impact-resistant carrying cases, to separate insurance policies when travelling, musicians know that good-quality instruments, tuned to their own particular tastes and needs, are a major factor in keeping them on top of their game.

As a singer, your voice is your instrument, and you need to treat it with even greater respect – after all, if you permanently damage it you can't just stroll down to the local music shop and buy a new one.

Most vocal problems start off small and are easy to deal with while they are still small. Unfortunately, most of us, male or female, adopt a very 'male' approach to vocal health: we ignore the early warning signs because we think we're invincible, then as the symptoms get worse we avoid getting a medical opinion because we fear hearing the worst, thereby greatly increasing our chances of hearing the worst when we are finally so ill or so voiceless we *have* to drag ourselves off to the doctor.

Even if the problem is minor (and as long as you're using your voice properly most ailments should be), recovery time is likely to be a lot longer if we don't get it sorted out soon enough.

Just as in every other branch of show business, the 'show must go on' philosophy applies to singers, and if the problem really is mild, such as a cold or regular sore throat, it is possible to 'sing through it' – say for a big gig that it's too late to cancel.

On the other hand, if it really is an important gig and you're serious about showing yourself off to best advantage, you need to ask yourself if a substandard vocal performance is going to be better in the long run than rescheduling the gig.

If you do make it through the gig, don't become over-confident. Consistently adjusting your vocal style to compensate for throat problems is just going to give you bad vocal habits and is quite likely to give you a new set of problems to add to ones you were trying to compensate for.

It can be a little bit easier if you are a band or group member: most audiences are very forgiving, especially when you are doing your best for them. John remembers seeing a rhythm and blues band with a female vocalist who had travelled all the way from the USA for a tour of Ireland. Unfortunately, somewhere over the Atlantic, Wanda the singer caught a throat infection. At the gig John saw, the guitarists all took it in turns to sing her songs, while Wanda saved what was left of her voice for two numbers at the end of the gig, both of which were met with thunderous applause . . . not unrelated to the fact that the previous 18 numbers had demonstrated that as vocalists the guys in the band were, well, really great guitarists.

Yet the whole gig had been carried off with such bonhomie and perseverance in the face of adversity that the audience were on side right from the start. It was one of those shows which was far more enjoyable and memorable than many involving vocalists with voices in full working order.

We've already mentioned in our chapter on performance the wisdom of being real with and communicating with your audience, so if you do choose to plough on with a show in the face of a throat bug or cold, it's probably best to tell the folks up front – but don't over-apologise for it or moan about it, just give the best show you can, and get medical attention as soon as you can afterwards.

If you are buying short-term medication to control the symptoms, make sure to mention to your pharmacist that you are a singer so they can suggest the type that will work best. Note too, that on the basis of 'if you're not well, you can't work', more and more singers, dancers and actors are joining old age pensioners in winter in getting the 'flu jab' as a matter of routine, rather than as treating it as an option like the general public.

Like every other part of our body, our voice carries a 'lifetime' guarantee, but only when we use it properly. Overuse and abuse are therefore at the root of almost all vocal problems.

But just in case you think this chapter mainly applies to thrash metal singers, it's worth pointing out that this overuse and abuse isn't always deliberate and can occur off stage as well as on.

By our nature we performers are theatrical – we are prone to live life bigger, faster and louder than most people, at least while we are in 'singer' mode. Unfortunately all of these qualities, particularly the 'loud' part, can do serious damage to our health and our vocals.

Speaking or singing too loudly can be a problem particularly when there is already vocal strain. Bear in mind that even if you're not naturally a loud person, showbusiness environments with loud music or instruments often involve you in having to shout over other noises . . . when you're not busy inhaling vast quantities of cigarette smoke.

Divas, male and female, may like to note that overemotional behaviour such as crying fits can also damage the vocal mechanism. But remember also that the danger lies in using the voice *improperly* rather than at a particular volume – singing or speaking too low or out of your range can do just as much damage as over-the-top loudness.

Listed below are some of the most common problems which affect singers, regardless of level of experience or area of music. You may want to check your own practice now, to save yourself a lot of grief later on:

Common problems for singers

Poor posture

Strictly speaking we don't sing with just our voice, we sing with our entire body, so if we don't carry our body properly it's going to affect the sound that comes out. Poor posture can range from slumped shoulders and collapsed chest area, making us strain for air, to exaggerated stiffness that causes tension in the vocal chords and everywhere else.

Poor posture is also, of course, a major indicator of nervousness and low self-esteem, so sprucing up this area of your physicality will have a beneficial effect not just on your voice but on your whole stage presence.

Poor breathing

It's no accident that most good singing teachers focus primarily on breathing. The accidents are reserved for singers who don't get this basic training – or those of us who stray away from it as our career progresses. Correct breathing has a positive effect not just on our voice, but on our general level of relaxation and confidence, and to complete the cycle, less stress in any area of our life leads to less stress on the vocal chords too.

Poor speaking habits

Guess what? It doesn't matter if we use our voice with perfect care and attention while singing if we then go and put it through the ringer every time we speak. Poor speaking habits can affect the sound and quality of our singing performance, through poor pronunciation and long hours talking on mobile phones are perfectly capable of straining our vocal chords just as efficiently as singing at the top of our voices in large rooms.

Poor self-control

Cigarettes, alcohol, drugs. Whether or not you use them is your own personal choice. What you don't get a choice in is the fact that everything you put into your body has an effect on the sound that comes out of it. And yes, that does include the touring band's staple diet of greasy fry-ups in transport cafés that Jabba the Hutt would refuse to eat in on the grounds of hygiene. It also applies to the 'serious recording artist' who lives on fizzy drinks and chocolate bars for a week because there's always 'just one more mix to record and every second we waste in the studio is costing us a fortune'.

Another area where singers have a tendency to push the envelope more than most is sleep. A good night's sleep is one of the most important factors in vocal and overall physical health, so if you do put in late nights at the studio or on the party circuit make sure you also allow time to catch up on lost sleep as soon as possible.

Besides affecting your vocal quality, fatigue will definitely affect your ability to give a good performance, and on long tours can play serious havoc with the brain without any help from other substances. At the time of writing, a major recording star in the middle of a long tour has just greeted a huge Canadian audience with 'It's really great to be in America', guaranteeing quite a few sleepless nights for her record company's PR people.

Vocal problems

Vocal problems can spring up at any time. Here are some of the symptoms to watch out for:

- Your chest feels tight, and you strain to reach notes you would usually find easy.
- Your breathing is short and holding notes is a problem.
- Your voice sounds hoarse, whether speaking or singing.
- Your voice is more fatigued after a gig and takes longer to recover than from just normal tiredness.
- You are coughing or needing to clear your throat more than usual.
- You have tickling or burning at the back of the throat.

As with all mechanical problems, the most important thing to do when you suspect your voice is not working properly is *stop using it*. And no, that doesn't just mean stop singing – talking and whispering are out too. Especially whispering, in fact, because any improper use of the voice whether loud or soft makes problems worse.

If you do choose to go on with a performance, conserve your voice as much as you can during any rehearsals, and once you're off stage, shut up.

As already mentioned, it may be that rest is all that is needed to solve the problem. It's also true that many of these symptoms could just mean you've caught a common cold or some other 'bug' that's going around, but just as a busy office needs to have technicians on 24-hour callout to sort out computer bugs while the rest of us are happy to sit and fume and wait for the helpline operator, if your voice is your livelihood no problem is too small not to have it checked out immediately.

It can also be possible to have most of the symptoms above and carry on singing for years – big mistake. If something is wrong, each performance will make it a little more wrong, and when you do finally have to get seen to, undoing the damage caused by neglecting the problem may be just as difficult as sorting the problem out in the first place.

When you do seek a medical opinion, beware that your average GP may not be expert in vocal problems related to singing. If you get the 'take two aspirins and call me in the morning' approach you'll need to get a referral to an ear, nose and throat specialist, preferably one who is used to working with singers.

Your singing teacher or vocal coach, if you have one, may be able to suggest such a doctor (and may well be able to give you good 'first aid' advice in the meantime). You can also ask friends in the singing business for recommendations. Many professional singers go to see specialists on an ongoing basis for check-ups, especially if they are in long-running shows or using their voices heavily.

Failing all that, you can try calling your local ear, nose and throat hospital directly (your local health authority should be able to tell you where it is). Another option is to phone the nearest music college and ask where they send ailing students.

Visiting a specialist is likely to cost, of course: it's for you to decide if protecting your greatest asset is a good investment.

Whether the problem is easily solved through rest and improved vocal technique or more severe, even involving (gulp!) surgery, be encouraged that the majority of problems are not career-threatening when treated properly and caught in time.

Like an athlete recovering from an injury, the speed at which a singer recovers will be determined by their focus and commitment to sticking to a prescribed regime of rest and exercise.

It's obviously a good idea to build good habits into your vocal programme right now to prevent problems happening in the first place.

Good vocal habits

Rest

Plan specific rest periods for your voice whether you feel you need to or not. Many top singers have a specific day of the week designated as a 'no speaking' day. No, you don't have to become a hermit – it's surprising how many other communication skills you can develop when you can't open your mouth. And we've already told you that successful performance is about far more than just your vocals, so the practice here can pay dividends for the rest of your stage act.

It may be difficult to get friends and family to go along with this at first, but if you explain the reasons and are consistent in sticking to your no-talking rule they can eventually be trained, and just like you, if they really need to communicate something they'll find another way.

Warm-up

Make sure you 'warm up' properly before any vocal performance – your singing teacher or vocal coach should have taught you appropriate exercises. If you've forgotten them or are too embarrassed to go back, you can buy practice tapes from music shops. But having someone knowledgeable check your technique once in a while is of definite benefit: you can't check if you're using your own voice properly, and avoid pushing or straining if you've never felt what healthy singing is supposed to be like in the first place.

Practice

Practise singing regularly even at times when you're not performing. Besides keep your voice in shape, you'll maintain a 'working fitness' in voice and performance that's easier to pull up to 'full match fitness' when you have an important gig.

You'll also get to know your own voice and be able to build on its strengths and work around its limitations.

Eating and drinking

Watch what you eat and drink prior to a performance. Most singers avoid eating for a least an hour or two before a show, and even many party animals avoid alcohol until after the gig. Room-temperature water or herbal tea is Julie's pre-show tipple of choice. The jury is out on strong mouthwashes, menthol or eucalyptus – some singers recommend them, especially for soreness, while others feel that in too strong quantities they can do more harm than good. The traditional throat remedy of using warm salt water may be a better bet.

Sound check

Try to make sure there's a small 'monitor' speaker facing you, or an earpiece available when you are on stage, especially if you are singing with a band. Not being able to hear your own voice – which you may well not be able to do without this assistance – will only drive you to push your voice more than you need to.

While we're on the subject of speakers, be aware that as well as vocal problems, many performers are at risk from hearing problems. Surprisingly, it's not the current obsession with ultra-loud live music which is the biggest threat, it's loud music played through badly tuned sound systems, of which unfortunately you'll encounter quite a few on the live circuit.

A proper sound check, therefore can be good not just for the quality of your performance but for the health of your own ears as well.

Warm-down

As with other physical activity, 'warming down' afterwards is a very important part of singing, and as with other physical activity, it's an important bit that quite often gets passed over for want of time.

Physical fitness

There are two kinds of people: those who enjoy sports, training and physical activity . . . and the other 99 per cent of the population. We've already mentioned above that the quality of your voice is directly affected by the condition of the rest of your body. It's also sad but true that show business is essentially fickle – if you miss a gig through poor health, the chances are somebody else will take over. Many of today's big names owe their 'break' to standing in for one of yesterday's big names who became indisposed. Yes, certain established stars have loyal fan bases who will put up with health hiccups and below-par performances for quite a while, but there really isn't any star name which is truly irreplaceable.

Buddy Holly's death may be referred to as 'The Day the Music Died', but it quite obviously marches on without him. The moral of the story is your health and fitness are career assets that only you can take responsibility for.

We've touched on image in another chapter, but it's worth saying a few words on the related subject of fitness. The personal trainer has over the last few decades become a major player in the entourage of every self-respecting celebrity, getting them toned up and perfectly proportioned for their next award-show appearance or music video. They may even feature in the star's bestselling workout tape.

For most singers at the entry end of the career ladder though, the main 'working out' personal trainers bring to mind is working out how on earth you can afford one.

Well, if you can afford one, by all means go ahead – looking after yourself properly will bring you a lot more benefits than many things you could be spending your hard-earned cash on. But just like an expensive keyboard with all the latest bells and whistles, or a state-of-the-art piece of music-editing software, a personal trainer or a more lowly gym membership is only going to improve your career if you actually use it.

First of all you need to set sensible goals for yourself. After all, your aim is to excel as an entertainer, not an athlete. You also need to opt out of the myth that it's only a certain size, shape and look that makes it in the world of show business. As we hope you've picked up by now, it's a certain *attitude* that leads to success in this or any other arena: that's the attitude that you will aim to be the best that you can be in every area of your career. Are you size 16 in a field where most other people seems to be size 8? Concentrate on being the best-looking, fittest size 16 you can be, and when your confidence starts to kick in, use it to get you down to size 14 if that's healthier for you.

From there you may be able to get to size 12 or size 10, and hopefully on the way you'll have realised that nobody sells extra records or puts on a better show because they've gone down two dress sizes. They succeed because they feel good about themselves and their talents, and the audience (which is usually made up of people just as insecure about their own image) feels good along with them because confidence is attractive.

Yes, we're addressing this bit mainly to female singers because women tend to have the most obvious concerns in this area, although it's our experience that most males in the public eye have the same concerns – they are just better at hiding them (or probably worse at expressing them).

And yes, dealing with weight and other physical problems is easier said than done. That's because most people just talk about it and don't actually do anything to rectify the situation.

Having made the commitment to take control of your health and fitness, not because you should, but because it will help your singing career, you can now decide how much time and money you can spend on this area.

Whether you can afford ongoing fitness training or not, it might be a good investment to at least book an assessment in the local gym, where you can have a proper training programme mapped out for you, based on the goals you want to achieve.

Many gyms offer 'off peak' membership, which can suit entertainers since our hours are different from everyone else's anyhow.

If you can't afford the gym, or even if you can but bore easily, you could try hooking up with likeminded friends for regular running or powerwalking sessions – although bear in mind that likeminded means 'committed'. The ideal training buddy is someone who'll tell you off if you slack off or don't show up. After all, that's basically what you'd be paying a personal trainer to do.

Another good investment would be to have a session with a nutritionist – diet being one of the major factors for good or ill in a person's fitness and general appearance. As we've already noted, the potential for musicians to miss meals and eat junk is far greater than in most other industries.

Expert advice can really help here: contrary to what fast food manufacturers would love you to believe, it is perfectly possible to eat cheaply, well and healthily if you know how. Self-invented 'diets' on the other hand are almost always useless at best or dangerous at worst. (Believe us, regular vomiting really, really does not help your vocal chords.)

Get professional advice on which vitamins and supplements to take – your average health shop has a huge array of concoctions all promising amazing benefits. Some of these products can be very good, compensating for missed meals, late nights and general physical and mental wear and tear. Some of them are a complete waste of money and possibly do more harm than good. We're not medical experts so we can't tell you which is which, but we can tell you it makes a lot of sense to get advice from somebody who can.

The trick with looking after your health isn't so much to do it at the beginning of your career – in fact, if you are sitting round waiting for the phone to ring it can be a welcome break to do an hour or two down at the gym. The real trick is to form a habit that you'll stick to when things get more hectic and you are living in hotel rooms or touring from gig to gig.

There is one way you can 'improve' your body without recourse to exercise or diet, and that's in the controversial area of cosmetic surgery. Michael Jackson is probably the best musical example of the extreme consequences of this course of action, but check out early photos of many singers in all branches of music against their current publicity shots and you'll see that quite a few have turned to the surgeon to make bits bigger or smaller and generally rearrange things they are not happy with.

Again, it's not for us to tell you how to spend your money. Indeed there are certain kinds of cosmetic surgery, such as getting your teeth fixed if they are not in great shape, that we'd heartily approve of. Just remember that unlike a new stage outfit, surgery is a lot more difficult to change if it doesn't have the desired effect.

Whatever you do don't use your career as an excuse to amplify existing doubts about your self-image. The big danger with cosmetic surgery is that it might just change your physical appearance and have the underlying doubts unaddressed. And it's those doubts that will hold your career back far more drastically than your physical appearance.

Which leads us quite neatly into the other area of health singers need to be aware of.

Mental health

The late Janis Joplin once described music stardom as making love to thousands of people and then going home alone. And she was lucky if she got to go home – for many working singers the end of the night is a lonely hotel room in a town whose name they've forgotten because it's the fifteenth night of their tour and all the road signs have blurred into one. It's not hard to see why addictions, affairs and severe personality disorders make frequent guest appearances in the history of music.

Established solo artists and bands may have their entourage, private jets and luxury coaches to make life easier, but the degree of excess that goes on at the upper end of the music market just proves the old adage that money and success don't change who you are, they just give you a chance to express who you are on a larger scale.

If you were screwed up before you made the big time, you'll now be able to afford bigger and more dangerous ways to demonstrate your screwiness, and attract a whole range of people who'll be happy to relieve you of your cash in exchange for screwing you up even further.

The time to start learning to cope with success is before you become successful, and given that the very nature of performing is that it's a lonely business, you need to become happy with the person you are behind all the glitz and glamour, because it's a person you may well be spending a lot of time alone with.

We've already mentioned the benefits of accepting who you are in terms of your talents and physical appearance. By all means aim to get the very best out of every aspect of your gifts and the way you present them – that's what this book is all about after all – but trust also that your God-given gifts are exactly the ones God felt you needed to fulfil your mission in life. (And He's what we'd call a showbiz manager with considerable experience.)

Here are some tips we've discovered that help keep a singer's life in perspective.

Keep life in perspective

Many people are waiting till they are successful to be free to give their singing career one hundred per cent. As we've been stressing throughout this book, if you don't aim for the best when you're starting out, you're unlikely to ever make it to the top.

Having said that, we suggest you give one hundred per cent to your singing when you're singing, and when you're involved with more 'mundane' activities like family, relationships, your hobbies or your day job you give them one hundred per cent too.

The principle cause of crack-up in any profession is the myth that if you get your career sorted out you'll get your life sorted out. The exact opposite is the case: get your life sorted out and you'll have a lot more positive energy to focus on your career. Be particularly careful to put your family life first, whether your family resembles the Osmonds or the Osbournes.

Remember that the people you are trying to appeal to are mostly not full-time singers. They have real lives . . . jobs, kids, relationships, ups and downs. To connect with them you have to experience all that stuff too, so you might as well enjoy it.

Another useful by-product of detaching yourself slightly from your singer persona is that it will help you cope better with rejections and setbacks. Unlike a writer whose book gets rejected, or even a songwriter whose tune doesn't make it to the final album selection – painful as those things can be – when we singers have a bad gig or fail to be chosen at an audition it's not just a song or a book, it's *us* who are being rejected and that can do quite a lot of psychological damage if we don't stop taking the whole thing so seriously.

Be careful of the company you keep

Performance is closely linked to ego. After all, you have to have some kind of ego to get up on stage and expect people to listen to you. Unfortunately, once people come off stage their egos don't necessarily go and sit quietly in the dressing room. It's also the nature of show business that not everybody succeeds, or at least succeeds to the level they feel their talent justifies. It follows, therefore, that not only are there usually a lot of egos flying round any showbusiness environment, many of them are angry, bitter and bruised, too.

Put that together with the fact that, by our nature, we performers tend to be highly concerned with what other people think, and it's quite easy to have our positive attitude diluted or even destroyed by getting drawn into the moaning, backstabbing and paranoia that can often be a part of showbusiness life. (Oops – that's John and Julie off most of the guest lists in town!)

You don't have to become Greta Garbo and shy away from all human contact, but it does make sense to be choosy about the company you keep, particularly during the inevitable knock backs and slow periods of a showbusiness career. They say opposites attract, but if you let your guard down you'll find negativity attracts other negative people like a magnet.

Mind you, there are also plenty of people both front and back stage that do have a positive attitude and can be a great source of support to each other – it just takes a bit more effort to hook up with them. But a good clue is that you'll usually find them busy working on their music, presentation or business approach rather than engaged in bitching sessions in the green room after a gig.

Don't believe your own publicity

Congratulations if you're still reading and haven't gone off to swap this book for *A Chartered Accountant's Guide to Finding Work*. The main reason we're painting a slightly negative picture of backstage life is that the whole nature of show business is to present an unnaturally rosy picture of life, which can trip up the unwary if they don't see beyond it to the reality. However, we wouldn't be writing this book if we didn't enjoy working in this industry, and we're sure bitchery, backstabbing and bitterness goes on in the world of chartered accountancy, too. One further pitfall which is slightly more prevalent in 'glamorous' industries, though, is the flipside of backstabbing: flattery and exaggerated praise. From 'air kissing' to 'Darling you were wonderful', the falseness of the showbusiness and media world is very easy to parody and very amusing when we see it sent up in shows like *Absolutely Fabulous*.

It can be a lot easier to fall for the real thing when we've been struggling to make our way as a singer and we're becoming increasingly desperate for a little support and affirmation. Just as you'll come across many people who'll put you down behind your back, you'll also find that there are lots of people ready to tell you exactly what you want to hear, particularly if your career is on the up, and they think a little flattery will help them sleep with you, get money from you or simply bask in your reflected glory.

The main danger of 'yes' people is the 'drip, drip' effect they have in eroding your own critical facilities. It's said that Elvis Presley knew his movie acting could do with improvement, but after a couple of years of everyone around him telling him how good he was he eventually gave up and went on making bad movies.

Start believing all the flattery, and inevitably your standards start to drop. As your standards drop your success rate will inevitably drop too . . . and surprise, surprise, when you've fallen flat on your face the only time you'll see your fair-weather friends is when they're stepping over you to get to their next target.

It's no secret that many of the singers who do stay focused and successful have a spiritual dimension to their lives, a belief that there's something bigger than them which prevents them getting caught up either in self-doubt or self-importance.

Whether or not you have 'someone up there' to talk to, it's one more reason for having a good team around you down here. Whether it's friends or family, hairdressers or sound engineers, or even other singers you've become friends with (yes, despite everything we've said good friendships do exist!), you need to surround yourself with people who like you for *you*, not because of your image or whether or not you're successful on any given day. A good team will tell you the whole truth: that means helping you identify things you do which work, so you can do more of them, and areas that need improvement so you can get busy improving them.

Even with a good team around, you need to keep your own focus and a clear head. Over the course of your career you'll be offered lots of advice. Some well meaning, some not, some from friends and family, some from fans, some from experts, some from other performers and books like this one: ultimately *you* are the only person who can decide which advice is going to work to your benefit.

Just as knowing your voice is the best way to maintain your vocal health, the best way to maintain mental stability is to know your own mind.

Safety

Having spent the whole chapter detailing how you can personally muck up your own health and career if you're not careful, it seems a shame to have to point out that even if you do take care of all these areas, you also need to be mindful of your personal safety as a working singer.

Particularly at the beginning of your career, you'll often be travelling alone to venues you've never been to, coming home late at night, or if you're on tour, staying in cheap guest houses or hotels.

The 'glamour' of show business can work its magic even in the smallest, dingiest pub. Unfortunately, sometimes this 'magic' can attract undesirable attention from audience members who don't understand that once the show is over you have a right to your privacy and personal space.

Obviously personal safety is particularly an issue for the female solo singer, but it's not unknown for male singers to attract unwelcome attention also, whether of the unwanted romantic kind or, more usually, from the large bloke who has decided his wife or girlfriend fancies you and has consequently decided to beat you up.

In an ideal world you won't be going to gigs alone of course, but even the most dedicated spouse, partner or circle of friends may not be available 24 hours a day, so male or female, it makes sense to apply 'blind date' safety principles to your singing gigs.

1 If you're going to a venue you haven't been to before, check the address beforehand and make sure you let someone know where you're going.
2 Take a mobile phone and make sure you have local cab numbers (yes, the venue management should sort out this for you, but you need to have a plan B).

3 Given the huge fluctuation in the quality of promoters and venues up and down the country it does no harm to keep an eye on fire exits, and the state of microphone leads and other electrical appliances you may be asked to use.

4 Even at the lower end of the showbiz ladder, anyone who appears on stage is automatically assumed to have money. Don't make it easy for thieves who would want to relieve you of yours. Also, don't take any valuables with you that you don't need for your show, and make sure there's somewhere secure in the venue to leave them while you're on stage. Often this does *not* mean the dressing room. Be particularly careful about leaving any instruments, stage costumes or props unattended.

5 As much as possible, aim to leave the venue as soon as you've finished the gig (and got paid, of course). Besides being safer, it makes you look more like a star.

If you have a business card or website address you can give it out as a contact for anyone who wants to talk to you after the gig. (Make sure your home address isn't on anything you're handing out freely.) If someone really is serious about offering you work, they'll hang on to the number and contact you. If the gig has gone well you may find punters want to buy you drinks – it's up to you whether you accept them, but make sure the combination of excitement and alcohol doesn't end up drowning your common sense. Safety concerns aside, never get into negotiations with anyone when you've been drinking – you don't want to find you've committed yourself to doing a Christmas season in the Outer Hebrides for the price of a pint!

6 It would be entirely foolish of us to pretend that casual sex isn't a frequent issue on the showbusiness circuit, and just as silly to deny that for more than a few singers it's one of their main motivations for getting involved in music in the first place. Whatever your own moral values, be aware that there are a whole lot of sexually transmitted diseases out there just waiting to seriously mess up your performance, whether in the bedroom or on the stage, and that the only 100 per cent reliable method of protection is using your brain in the first place.

And yes, sex can be and is used as a method of career advancement – but bear in mind that if someone is advancing your career purely on the basis that you are having sex with them (or behaving as if you might), advancement can come to a very sudden stop when they get what they want and their attention turns elsewhere. And in show business attention spans tend to be extremely short.

As we said at the beginning of this chapter, we've tried to set out some sensible and practical health guidelines without getting too preachy – and if our overall message is that 'high standards off stage lead to high standards on stage', then we hope by now we're preaching to the converted.

In our final chapter, we're going to look at the area of the working singer's career where high standards are the most crucial – and also the one where many singers find those standards most difficult to maintain. Now that you've had some pointers on your own health, let's explore how you can get your business affairs in order once and for all and give yourself the security of a healthy career.

Chapter Seven

No Business Like Show Business

The business of being a working singer

Mick Jagger once said that the reason 'pop music' was so called is that after the initial success, everything goes 'pop' and disappears. We've met enough casualties of this phenomenon to suggest that this applies across every other genre of music too.

In our chapter on health we mentioned that performers are notoriously bad at looking after their physical well-being. It has to be said that the danger of messing up the health aspect your career is only surpassed by the danger inherent in not paying proper attention to the business health of your career

One of the saddest things about meeting singers who are broke, bitter or just about ready to quit is reflecting on the fact that they were once full of the same excitement, dreams and sheer joy in using their singing gifts as many of the beginners reading this book.

More often than not, their current circumstances are a direct result of taking their eye off the ball in the business area (or perhaps never realising there was a ball to keep their eye on in the first place).

On a more positive note, there are many performers who have long since passed their 'heyday' or have never even had a particular heyday, who are nonetheless happy, prosperous and regularly in work precisely because of careful management of their business affairs.

We hope it's clear from the general tone of this book that we love the music world – neither of us would have worked in it for so long in our differing capacities if we didn't. On the other hand we'd be very disingenuous if we pretended that the music/showbusiness industry didn't have a well-earned reputation for being very hard-nosed and occasionally downright ugly beneath the glitzy surface.

A quick overview of musical history will also confirm that while not everyone you will come across is a shark or a charlatan, there are enough of these people about that if you don't keep your wits about you, you are liable to get badly bitten.

Once you're out on stage your success or failure is generally down to you, your talent and how you relate to your audience. But getting onto that stage, and what happens when you come off it, involves you interacting with the showbusiness and music industries as a whole, and in order to do so effectively it's very important that you have a realistic and up-to-date understanding of how they work.

That's not something we can cover in detail in one chapter. It's not even something we could cover in a whole book – but as with our tips in every other chapter on performance, we can bring some issues to your attention here and hope that you will find out more about them through practice, experience and further reading. Unlike our other chapters, though, these points are not ones which will help your career the more you pursue them: in the area of business, it's what you don't learn that can hurt your career and your life in very real ways.

Actually, before we start ranting about 'nasty music business people and how they might rip you off', it's worth putting on record that when it comes to business many singers we know don't need any help in being ripped off – they are perfectly capable of shooting themselves in the foot all by themselves.

The same passion for music and joy in performing we mentioned in our introduction can be all-consuming, certainly far more attractive than more mundane activities like balancing cheque books, filing receipts or going to meetings with the bank manager.

Our education system is such that children increasingly get pushed into different areas as they develop . . . and pushed out of other ones. It's not completely true that people who are naturally gifted in creativity and performance are not good at business, finance and organisation, but a belief that this is true is certainly a common one that society seems to reinforce.

The music industry also does its best to reinforce it, for its own good reasons. One of the most common pieces of advice we hear experienced musicians give to beginners when recounting their own (usually unhappy) stories is 'Always remember this about the music business – it's all about business'.

We hear what they say, but we'd disagree. The music business is all about music: singers, songwriters, musicians and the magic that happens when they put their creative talents to work. But just like the coffee industry or the tobacco industry, the people who make the most money from these talents generally are not the people who 'farm the soil', but managers, executives, distributors . . . the people who have made a business out of what is essentially a creative art.

Does this mean all these people are bad? Not at all – but it does point up the fact you need to consciously make your singing a business at its source to reap maximum benefit from it financially and also to give you the freedom to do the creative and performance work that comes from your heart.

With this in mind it's a very useful exercise to cast aside the myth that there's anything mysterious or difficult about successful business practice or that singers are any less qualified to do it than anyone else.

Yes, there are plenty of managers, agents and accountants who operate with absolute honesty and integrity, and there also performers who use the 'but I'm not good at business' excuse when they actually mean 'I'm too lazy to learn about business'.

But there are also plenty of people ready, willing and able to convince you that you really need their services to further your career, and who will then take a percentage of your earnings or your self-esteem in exchange for doing something you could do perfectly well yourself

The second myth to get rid of is that show business is essentially different from any other business: if you were to take the principles we looked at in our marketing chapter for producing promotional material and sending it to a targeted customer base and apply it to any other service, from carpentry to hairdressing, it would work just as well. (Obviously carpenters wouldn't necessarily get extra work by sending out 8″ × 10″ glossy photos of themselves, although if any carpenters reading this want to try, please let us know how you get on.)

Similarly carpenters have to budget, prepare business plans and employ staff as their business expands, and those are exactly the same issues you need to deal with if your business happens to be singing.

In our introduction we spoke about your having an overall vision for your career, and this is essentially your business plan. It sets out your goals for what you want to achieve in your career and helps you judge each decision you make against your ultimate goal, and if you find your career has gone off track, referring back to your plan will help you identify what's gone wrong and what you need to do to fix it.

Although there are many different kinds of singer, at many different levels, from solo artist to band member, to 'name' act with a full complement of agents and managers, we've approached most of this book from the point of view of the individual singer at the start of their career, doing everything themselves.

As we've said before, it's always good to do everything yourself at least once so that when you employ someone else to do it, you know what they're supposed to be up to and if they're doing it properly. This is particularly true in the business arena so we'll start off by looking at some of the areas you need to address from your own point of view, and then take a look at the pros and cons of some of the people you can link up with to help you manage them.

Finances

'I don't care about the money, I'm in it for my art', is a common cry of singers, actors, dancers and creative talents of all types. Unfortunately, the reason the vast majority of performers cite for not being able to pursue their career at the level they would like is chronic lack of money. Yes, there are fortunes to be made in the music business, and despite what we've written above about the unbalanced nature of the industry, singers do make them, too, but equally there are a lot of singers living precariously from gig to gig or working in energy-sapping part-time or full-time jobs to earn the time and finances to work on their singing.

We're not for a minute advising you to throw up your existing job if you have one and embark today on a full-time singing career. Nor is there anything wrong with supplementing your singing career with part-time work: if you're hoping to get other people to invest in your talent, you need to be willing to invest some time in it too, even if it's working in the local telephone sales centre.

But like all careers, the key element in the success of a singing career is initially not so much how much money is coming into the business but how well you manage the money that comes into the business.

Recent surveys have thrown up frightening statistics about how badly the average member of the public manages their money, with levels of poverty and debt rising all the time. As already mentioned, the performer mentality lends itself to flamboyant overspending in all the wrong areas even in the absence of actual money, and things are not made easier by the existence of easy credit and aggressive consumer advertising.

For singers there's another temptation: the fact that no matter how badly we manage our money there's always the hope that just around the corner will come the 'big break', the gig where we are discovered, the major record deal, the number one hit record that will end our money worries for ever. Well, who are we to say it won't happen (and if it does, please mention our book in all your TV interviews), but using the possibility of good luck tomorrow to avoid managing your money sensibly today, is the road to ruin – and many people who *did* get the big break, the big contract and the big hit record have only gone on to prove that if you can't handle money when you have a little of it, you will mess things up on an even more spectacular level when you get a lot of it.

Step number one in managing our finances is, at least for a great many of us, to bite the bullet and see where we actually are financially. This is particularly so if there are a large number of unopened brown envelopes piling up on the carpet. Take a deep breath and open them, and make a list of everything you owe and everything that is regularly coming in, whether from your day job or from your singing. (If there isn't a regular income figure out a monthly estimate.)

Now subtract your monthly outgoings total from your monthly income and you are left with your disposable income. This is the money you have available to invest either in enjoying yourself or in furthering your career.

What if you don't have any money left – or worse, have a large minus figure? Thanks to the wonders of high-interest credit cards and other 'easy' loans it is now perfectly possible for performers, a species once ranked somewhere between kamikaze pilots and bomb-disposal crews as poor credit risks, to get access to more borrowed money than is good for them . . . and thanks to the average singer's capacity to live life in the fast lane, it is equally possible to get into a huge amount of debt extremely quickly.

If this is the case, take heart: the first step in dealing with a problem is to recognise it. The next step is to ruthlessly get things sorted out as soon as you possibly can. It is very difficult to carry yourself like the major star that you are if you have to step over a mountain of unopened brown envelopes every time you want to go out your front door.

There are now several charities dealing with debt management who will help you work out a budget and negotiate a repayment scheme with your creditors. Try these organisations first in preference to commercial debt-management companies who perform exactly the same function but charge you for the privilege, thereby increasing rather than decreasing your debt.

Cut down on all but essential spending, and no that doesn't mean compromising on your performance style: start home cooking with simple ingredients and it's amazing how soon the money saved from all those takeaway meals that you would normally have mounts up enough to cover a new backing track or getting your stage outfits dry cleaned.

Even if you do have money coming in from singing jobs or other employment and aren't up against the wall financially, good money management is a useful habit to acquire: for one thing entertainment income by its nature fluctuates considerably, so even with a run of well-paid gigs it's a good idea to put something aside for drier periods.

You'll also need to put something aside for tax, because whether your singing income is full time or an extra, it's all taxable, and you need to declare it – not least because the venues and companies employing you will be declaring it when they do their end-of-year accounts. While the Inland Revenue are not monsters, they are very strict about tax returns and they will hold out for every penny you owe them, not to mention charge high rates of interest if you fall behind.

If accounts really aren't your strong point (and even if they are), the time and grief you save by hiring an accountant to make your returns may more than justify the cost (which, like a lot of your showbusiness expenditure, you can claim for). If you do get an accountant it pays to get one who knows show business. Since a singer's income tends to be sporadic, a good accountant may be able to (legally) spread payments over two years to make things a bit less painful. More and more performers are dispensing with accountants altogether and getting a software package to do the figures for them. Whatever path you choose, just make sure those accounts get done.

However, having an accountant is no excuse for not keeping an overview of your own financial affairs: quite a lot of the high-profile financial disasters that have befallen well-known recording artists have been caused not so much by losing money as by not keeping an eye on their money in the first place. One major rock star famously got 'stung' by having vast amounts of money siphoned off by his accountant without his even noticing, keeping comedians in gags for years afterward. But those of us who can't keep tabs on even our small income now, need to learn the lesson too, before the last laugh is on us.

Managers and agents

It should be clear from all we've written so far that we consider good business management essential for the working singer. Nowhere are we suggesting, however, that it's actually fun. We've also noted already that the goal of most singers and musicians is simply to be on stage or in the studio doing what they do best, and all the promotion, negotiation and business hassle is just a means to get them out there.

It's no surprise, then, that the idea of having someone take over your life and career and 'make it all happen' for you is extremely attractive. Indeed, agents and managers have become as much a status symbol for the successful artist as the stretch limo waiting for them after the gig.

'What you need is a good agent' and 'With the right management you could be big', are both phrases you'll come across sooner or later in your career, and for the up-and-coming artist or the singer who is finding it tough out there on their own, such statements are likely to be music to the ears. Unfortunately, often the people uttering them are *bad* agents and the *wrong* managers, and if you don't want your career going down a cul-de-sac that not even your stretch limo can get you out of, it's vital you learn to tell the good from the bad.

When considering agent or management deals, whether they have been offered to you or you have sought them out yourself, it's important to remember one important fact: as a working singer you are the boss and chief executive of your own company. The vision and dream for the company is all yours, and anyone else you bring on board to further those dreams works for you.

Nor in most cases are 'your people' working for you for the good of their health. Whether the pay-off is a percentage of your earnings or the credit for making you a star, it's a simple fact that any business relationship in entertainment is a two-way street. That's not necessarily wrong or bad, but before you enter into a relationship with anyone, you both need to be very clear on exactly what the two of you are hoping to get out of it.

A good start would be to understand the difference between managers and agents, particularly because in this country people (including agents, managers and artists) tend to use the two interchangeably. The situation isn't made any easier by the fact that there isn't a standard definition of what managers or agents do, any more than there's a typical artist/management arrangement.

A singer might be the only act on the books of a determined individual who keeps them employed through sheer hustle and hard graft. Then again, they might be signed by a large corporate entertainment agency that books them into holiday camps, cruise ships and hotels which are owed by the parent company of the same agency. Equally, there are several major music stars who are managed by mums, dads or in some cases their grown-up sons and daughters. (There are also lots of stories of major stars who have been ripped off by their own family members, so it's worth pointing out that adhering to strict business principles applies doubly when dealing with people you're close to.)

Loosely defined, a manager is someone who 'maintains' a business. Whether it's a commercial company or a showbusiness 'act', the manager's job is to look at the existing goals of the company (i.e. your vision) and guide you towards them as effectively as possible.

An agent's job is to take over any negotiations involved along the way.

In practice, every manager and agent operates differently. Some are extremely 'hands on', directing every aspect of an artist's career from what they sing to what they wear, to whom they're seen with. Others don't get involved in the artistic side of the singer's career at all, only stepping in to negotiate deals or sort out contracts that the artist has already instigated themselves.

Which kind of arrangement suits you is down to your own personality and what you want out of your career. It's true to say, though, that one of the primary functions of an agent or manager in an artist's life is to be moaned about.

If there's not enough work coming in the agent isn't marketing us properly. If there's lots of work coming the manager is earning their pound of flesh off the back of our blood, sweat and tears. From the agent and management side of the coin we have heard it said that working with performers is like having a spoiled child, except that occasionally even spoiled children give back some love and affection.

Ultimately, we get the agents and managers we deserve, so here are some pointers to help you find a good one.

There are basically two routes to finding representation. Route number one is for you to make the decision that you need some help in this area. If this is the case it's very important to work out exactly what you want the agent or manager to do for you. As we've said at length, the vague dream that someone is going to take over your career and make things happen by magic is just that – a pipe dream. Just as different artists have different strengths, managers have different strengths and different areas of expertise, too. For instance, if your ambitions lie in the recording industry, a manager who specialises in live acts, no matter how successful, may not be the best person to work with.

How do you find the right manager or agent for you? By keeping an eye on what's going on in the business, by finding out who is looking after the most successful acts in your own chosen field, and by applying the same market research and detective work as you do to promoting yourself to audiences and the rest of the industry.

If you find someone you think might suit, it's then your task to convince them that you suit them by sending them demos, inviting them to gigs and otherwise making yourself stand out from the crowd.

It goes without saying of course that the bigger and more successful the manager or agency, the more successful the acts they already have on their books and the less inclined they may be to deal with beginners who may not bring them as high a percentage as one of their name acts. On the other hand, performers get old and musical fashions change, so a smart entertainment company is always on the lookout for 'the next big thing'. Or at least someone they can transform into 'the next big thing'.

If you manage to attract interest from a number of managers at the same time, you need to do some thinking. Will you get more attention from a manager with a small number of acts than from someone who has a lot of big names of which yours is very far down the list? Managers and agencies who handle really big names do, however, often have the power to put together package deals whereby clients get one of their big names with a support bill composed of up-and-coming acts managed by the same company. Every deal has its pros and cons, and knowing exactly what you want out of the deal is the best way to work out which is which.

The other way to find a manager or agent is when they are the ones pursuing you.

Very few performers, even at the lower end of the entertainment spectrum, get many gigs under their belts without someone coming up afterwards and offering to make it all happen for them. It's quite possible the offer will come from a legitimate professional, of course, for the reasons we mentioned above – successful managers and agents do keep an eye on showcases and talent shows looking for acts they can develop and add to their roster. And if you're working as hard at your craft as we hope you are, there's no reason why you shouldn't be the one to catch their eye.

Unfortunately, there are also corrupt, deluded and just plain weird people out there, and sadly there are also singers who have had such a rough time of it that an expression of interest or shred of hope from any source, no matter how unlikely, will lead them right up the garden path.

So however you come across a potential agent or manager, bear these points in mind:

Does this person look professional? Do they have an office, a decent business card, a proper suit . . . clean fingernails? Sorry to sound ruthless, but any manager or agent you take on will be the first point of contact between you and the entertainment industry. More to the point, someone who can't manage to create success for themselves isn't very likely to manage it for you.

Does this person have a track record? More than any other business, show business is the main epicentre of the world's false promises. Before you get too closely involved with any business associate, check out that what they're telling you or promising you is true. How do you do that? As we've been telling you all along, *you* need to become enough of an expert in your chosen area to able to work out if what they're telling you is true. This is particularly the case if you are approached by someone who may be genuinely successful, but in a different branch of music from the one you're hoping to succeed in. Yes, it's true that a professional is a professional, but trying to promote an R & B singer when your background is in folk music doesn't make things any easier.

Does this person believe in *you*? Let's say you've been approached by the manager of a top rock band who's looking for some new acts. So it's all systems go on the professional front – after all, the guy's a millionaire with an office full of PAs, stylists and men in suits. The track record is there too, not to mention the real records – he's got a least 10 gold ones on his studio wall. The management contract is on the table. So what are you waiting for?

Well, what you *should* be waiting for (besides for your lawyers to finish checking the contract, as you'll see in the next section) is some evidence that your benefactor isn't just interested in signing a hot act, he (or she) is interested in signing *you*.

Show business is a highly competitive field, and building a career takes time, money and expertise (note we said a 'career', not a 'one-hit wonder'). It is very difficult to sell something you're not personally enthusiastic about. You need to be sure that the people representing you are enthusiastic about something more than just your money-making potential, so that not only will they sell you, they'll sell your vision and hang in there with you if it takes a little while to get the mix just right. Being clear in this area is even important if *your* only goal for your music is to make as much money as possible from it: getting taken up by a major agency or record label and then dropped when the 'project' doesn't work out can do more damage to the confidence of the singer at the centre of the project than not getting signed up at all.

There is a flip side to the 'belief' issue, of course: just as you may feel you're not making the progress you deserve, your friends, family and whatever fan base you've acquired will certainly feel that way too, and it's quite possible that if nobody else steps forward one of them may take on the role of agent or manager, officially or unofficially.

Can it ever work? Well, stranger things have happened. While you should certainly insist on a professional approach, the lack of a track record needn't be a terminal failing if the person is willing to admit what they don't know and then put enough effort into learning fast. They'll certainly get further than someone who pretends to know it all but doesn't. And we would never underestimate the power of someone who really believes in you – just remember that management based on an existing personal or fan relationship may mean that neither of you is objective enough about the project to address what needs to be improved or changed to guarantee success.

Be particularly wary of the well-meaning friend or even the well-meaning professional who happily jumps into sorting out your career as a way of avoiding their own personal and professional problems. It happens a lot and, like 'rebound relationships' of any other sort, is guaranteed to end in further hurt and resentment on both sides.

It's also sadly true that if the whole relationship goes pear-shaped, as agent/artist relationships are wont to do, your personal relationship probably won't survive either.

And the topic of relationships, whether successful or un-successful, brings us to one of the music business's thorniest subjects.

Contracts

We could wrote a whole book on the ins and outs of show-business contracts. Indeed, some showbusiness contracts are very nearly long enough to fill up that book all by themselves.

But long or short, all the advice we can offer you can be summed up in one single sentence: *Never sign any contract or agreement unless you understand exactly what you are signing.* And even then, don't sign it until you've got professional advice. And after you've got professional advice leave it in a drawer for a few days until you can look at it with a clear head.

Think we're exaggerating? Then you've never seen, as we have, the artists who've put out one record and then lost their record deal, only to find they'd signed a contract that made them liable to pay for all the promotion, production costs, limousines and launch parties that were involved in their brief spell in the limelight. Or the groups who had a string of top 10 hits but don't get a single penny because they signed away the rights in the original contract (it's not unusual to unwittingly sign away the group name also, so that when you get stroppy the management can sack you and replace you with someone else).

Our personal favourite story is of the soul legend who had one of the biggest dance hits of the last three decades, which probably plays in a nightclub or on the radio somewhere in the world every five minutes. Not only does she not get any royalties from it – the record company says she owes them money.

Is it all the fault of nasty, evil music-business people? Well, it's true that a lot of the corruption and manipulation that goes on behind the scenes would make Darth Vader blush . . . but as we've said before, many singers don't need any outside help getting themselves into trouble – a combination of eagerness for the big time, or desperation for the big break, leads them to accept the first offer or *any* offer they get.

The simple fact is that any contract you're offered by a management company, a record company or a promoter is designed to protect *their* interests, so you need to have it checked out by someone who can protect *your* interests. Just as an ordinary GP is the wrong person to bring vocal problems to, your average high-street lawyer is not going to be equipped to deal with the ins and outs of music contracts, and – no matter how tight money is – running the contract past a qualified showbusiness lawyer is an investment you'll be glad you made.

(Under no circumstances use a lawyer recommended by the company you are negotiating with . . . yes, we once thought we'd never have to offer such obvious advice, too.)

Oh, and when you do get a lawyer to look over your contract, make sure you have a contract – or at least a letter of agreement – with your lawyer too. Basically, you need to get in the habit of putting *every* relationship you have in writing. It may seem a million miles away from the business of singing, but you'll find your singing career is a lot less hassled if you and all of your business associates are singing off the same sheet.

People who need people

Okay, if we were you we'd be getting a bit worried right about now – managers, lawyers, accountants, how are you going to afford all that lot at the beginning of your career?

Well, it's all a case of believing in yourself enough to make whatever investment of time and money you can afford, to get the best-quality people around you.

It's not necessarily true that the best people are the most expensive, but in the areas of management, legal and financial support it pays to get the best services you can find.

There are times, however, when you may be able to find good people without paying a fortune. For instance, you may come across a talented songwriter who needs a good vocalist to demo some tracks: if you can oblige you may get some studio time, or even some specially tailored songs in return. Or there are plenty of talented fashion designers around who are trying to build their own careers and get exposure just as you are trying to build yours. Again, you may be able to work out a deal of mutual benefit whereby you get some classy stage outfits and they get their designs shown off in a glamorous and high-profile environment.

The key thing to bear in mind is that you must only work with people who, whether experienced or not, are at the same level or higher in professionalism and ability in their own fields as you are in yours.

With the best will in the world, the weakest link in any chain is the one that brings everyone else down to their level. Just as the classiest stage outfit in the world will look cheap if the photos of it are taken by your granny with her disposable camera, a group which features Eric Clapton and BB King on guitar, Elton John on piano and Candi Staton, Whitney Houston and Julie Payne on vocals will still sound rubbish if it has John Byrne playing the drums (although the cartoons on the CD cover will be pretty good).

On the other hand, get someone who is as talented as you are and who is anxious to prove themselves, and you may get even more effort put into your stage outfit or the production of your demo track than an established professional would expend.

However, the rule we've just been going on about applies even more in this 'barter' situation: *Get every agreement, no matter how informal, down in writing.*

This is for the protection of all parties involved. For instance, what happens if you do a great vocal on someone's demo track and they write you a hit song . . . only an existing chart act hears the song and wants to record it themselves? Or you've been wearing clothes by an up-and-coming young designer and that image boost has helped bring you to the attention of a top management company, but as part of the management contract the company wants to have you styled by an established designer?

It's unlikely you'll get anywhere in your career without being faced with hard decisions along the way. While writing things down doesn't guarantee you'll always be left with a good feeling, it does keep your reputation for fair play intact, and stops you getting completely ripped off if the other party's reputation isn't as important to them.

Of course, all your business relationships may not be equal or 'one to one'. Hard enough as it is to manage your own life, you may well find yourself having to manage others' too.

As you start getting more and more important gigs you may want to put together your own backing band. Now instead of just getting yourself to the gig you've got up to five or more people to keep an eye on (and believe us, musicians need more 'keeping an eye on' than most people). You need to be sure that they understand exactly what's expected of them. Also you need to have on paper how much they're each getting paid and when, because no matter how well or badly the show goes we can guarantee that the musicians will be looking for their money immediately afterwards.

It may seem cold to reduce everything to written agreements at the point where everything is based on mutual goodwill and enthusiasm, but believe us it avoids a lot of bad feeling and bitterness further down the road.

I'd like to thank my fans . . .

Throughout this chapter we've talked about singing in the context of other service industries. Your voice, your shows, your records, are the product. Your self-promotion and marketing is your advertising campaign. And your fans are your customers.

Right now your fan base may consist of your mum, your dog and the imaginary audience you sing to with your hairbrush in front of the bedroom mirror. But take your career seriously, try some of the advice in this book and build up your all-important mailing list and it may not be long before you have a genuine following. The only snag is that they may follow you into parts of your life you'd rather they didn't.

In most other businesses, customers only have access to the product during business hours, but in show business if you're not careful you are on show all the time. At the early stage of your career, unless you are very unusual, getting recognised off stage and being asked for an autograph or a photo is a big boost to the ego – an affirmation that at last you are getting somewhere. Sooner or later though, fans are going to want to talk to you when you're *not* all that keen to see them. Say when you're on your way to the shops with no make-up on, or you're collecting your kids from school, or when you're stuck on a cruise ship with a terrible hangover and nowhere to hide for the next three weeks. Nor will the people who like your music necessarily be the same people you'd choose as your friends. They may be a lot older than you. They may be a lot younger than you. They may, quite frankly, be a lot smellier than you.

At times like this, remembering that they are your customers, and the ones who ultimately pay your wages, is very important. In most cases fans are very pleasant and genuinely want to express appreciation for what you do, and we hope you'll be equally gracious, even when you're asked the same questions over and over again. Being nice not only costs nothing, it can pay dividends in future ticket and record sales.

On the other hand, you have just as much right to privacy as anyone working in any other business. As noted in the chapter on personal safety, be very careful about giving out personal details or inviting fans into your personal life. Besides making good common sense, it makes good business sense: the very fact of being a 'fan' of someone means you want them to be special and perfect, an 'ideal', and getting to know that person, warts and all, usually just spoils the illusion.

Of course if you've read the book this far, you'll know 'stardom' is something of an illusion, anyhow – most stars are ordinary people who had a vision and applied some hard, focused work to making it a reality. From taking care of your voice to taking care of business, we promised you a run through of the building blocks of a successful singing career. No matter how big your favourite star in whatever branch of music, check out the history of their career and you'll find that they've applied most of the basic information we've provided in these pages, often after several years of learning the hard way.

The one element we can't teach you, of course, is 'star quality', but we can assure you everyone has it. The question is whether you're prepared to put in the hard work, long hours and personal sacrifice required to discover your unique brand of it and start using it.

If you are, we've included a resource section at the end of the book to give you lots more information and avenues to explore. The best and most successful singers always stay ahead of the game, and this is a game where the rules are forever changing.

One thing that won't change, though, is that out of all of the hundreds and thousands of people who dream of being a singer there will only be a small number with the talent and determination to turn that dream into reality. If you're one of those people, we hope this book has helped make that determination just a little bit stronger.

Keep us in touch with how you're getting on through our website: www.webtoonist.com. Hey, we may even pop up at one of your gigs if you let us know where you're playing.

But whether we ever see you live, or hear you on the radio, know that there's a place in the centre of a stage somewhere that God has put your name and yours alone on.

Are you determined enough to step up and take it?

Your audience is waiting and the spotlight's on you.

Case Studies

Two working singers

All the techniques and tips on the preceding pages work. We know because we have seen them put into practise successfully. Of course you're not going to find out if they work for you until you try them too. Just to inspire you further, we've persuaded two of our singing heroes to share their own career stories in detail with us. We've chosen Sheila Ferguson and Dec Cluskey not just because they are friends of ours, nor simply because they both have strings of hit records under their belts (the goal of every beginning singer), but because they have each translated their abilities into successful and flourishing long-term careers.

You'll see how early determination to make the most of every opportunity has translated into a lifelong refusal to settle for anything less than excellence. And you'll also see the rewards this attitude brings. But let them tell you about it in their own words. Ladies first . . .

Sheila Ferguson

Sheila Ferguson is a lot more than just a soul music legend – she is also an accomplished actress, writer and a world authority on soul food, African America's traditional cuisine. Born in Philadelphia, USA, Sheila at first had ambitions to be a psychologist. However, a successful solo singing career put these ambitions on hold. By 1965 she was recording regularly for the Swan Record label under the tutelage of doo wop legend Richard Barrett, cutting a number of highly regarded singles including 'Little Red Riding Hood', 'How Did That Happen' and 'Heartbroken Memories'. As well as appearing at all the top music venues, including the Apollo (where she shared the bill with Marvin Gaye), Sheila was, most unusually for a female vocalist of that era, already writing her own songs.

While Richard Barrett was working with Sheila he was also developing a female vocal group called the Three Degrees. A strong friendship had developed between Sheila and the other group members, who often sang back-up on her records, just as she provided extra harmonies on theirs, sometimes even standing in for missing Degrees at live dates. When one of the original members left, it was no surprise that Sheila was asked to join for good.

The Three Degrees, with Sheila as lead, became the most successful female group of the 1970s, spearheading the rise of the Philadelphia International label and the Philly Sound, with a string of worldwide hits such as 'TSOP (The Sound of Philadelphia)' (with MFSB), 'Dirty Ol' Man', 'Take Good Care of Yourself', 'Year of Decision' and the Kenny Gamble/Leon Huff classic 'When Will I See You Again'. Just as renowned for their dynamic stage act as for their glamour and vocal excellence, the Three Degrees toured all over the world, attracting a huge and loyal fan base in countries ranging from Japan to Australia and, of course, the UK. The girls have appeared on most of the world's top TV shows, ranging from cult American sitcom *Sandford and Son*, starring the late Redd Foxx, to the primetime special on British TV broadcast from London's Royal Albert Hall. The group also made an explosive appearance in the Oscar-winning Gene Hackman/William Freidkin movie *The French Connection*.

In the 1980s the Three Degrees were still topping the charts with discs such as 'My Simple Heart', working with Disco King Georgio Moroder. Hits like 'The Runner' and movie theme 'The Golden Lady' showed Sheila taking more of a hand in production and songwriting duties, but as the mother of twins she found it less and less easy to balance family life with recording and touring, so in 1985 Sheila finally left the group.

After leaving the Three Degrees, Sheila became much sought-after as a solo performer. She reached the top of the corporate circuit. Sheila sings in six languages. She tailors each of her shows to fit each individual audience. Sheila then made the cross-over into acting. Her first venture was to star in her own UK-based sitcom, *Land of Hope and Gloria*, produced by Thames television.

Soon after that, Sheila decided that the natural progression was to combine the two art forms – singing and acting – and she went into musical theatre. She took London's West End by storm, starring in the hit musical *Soul Train*. Sheila also took a cameo role in the West End musical *Always*, and added sparkle to the sell-out disco show *Oh! What a Night*.

Sheila Ferguson's gift for the gab has always kept her in high demand for special television appearances and she is still a favourite of the royals all across Europe. It is said that HRH Prince Charles is still her number one fan.

At the time of writing, she is working on several new TV shows, a Broadway musical and a major movie project. Her website, www.sheilaferguson.com, is one of the most highly regarded performers' sites on the Web, and an object lesson in how to tailor marketing material to reflect a performer's image.

Dec Cluskey

Dec Cluskey, lead singer of the Bachelors ('The Original Irish Boyband'), has appeared with almost every showbiz legend in the world, from Judy Garland through to Ant and Dec, via Brian May, Rick Wakeman, Tom Jones, Neil Diamond, Englebert, Sammy Davis Jr, Bob Hope, Morecambe and Wise, Tommy Cooper, Tony Bennett, Cliff, the Beatles, and even the Pope! Here's what he has to say about his career.

> *Where we were*
> My mum was not too pleased when I gave up a position in the Chief Civil Engineer's Department of CIE (the Irish equivalent of British Rail) to have a go at the music industry in the UK. I had read civil engineering and this was my first (and last) 'proper' job. Yes, we had had a fantastically successful career playing mouth organs (okay, don't laugh) since I was 12! The first TV show we did was the famed Ed Sullivan Show on US television. Not bad for the first one! Then we appeared on the opening night of Irish Television in 1961 – a great honour.
>
> Tried the 'big time' in the UK for a few days . . . *Opportunity Knocks* – what a flop! Then tried it for four weeks . . . boy, was my headteacher miffed when I disappeared for that length of time!

Then the big step

We heard whispers that a big 'London' agent was interested in us – Philip Solomon, who discovered Ruby Murray, Lena Zavaroni . . . the list is endless. At that time he wanted us to tour with Nina and Frederik (who had a chart hit with a song called 'Little Donkey') for five weeks . . . great.

So we ended up in England

After the five weeks? Broke, forlorn, homesick, destitute . . . the third member of the band went back to Ireland, leaving me and my brother Con to go it alone.

Coincidence?

We found out that the landlady knew a guy called Frank White who just happened to be a relation of my father! Uncanny or what? Quick phone call. '*Leave it with me for an hour.*' Sure enough we got to see him and blow me, we were up and running: three shows for that weekend. First, call Mum – we needed our guitars, double bass and amplifier, double quick! Should we call the third singer back from Ireland? Yes/No? Yes/No? . . . oh, all right then, toss the coin. We ended up a few months later in a summer season in Arbroath, Scotland. Salary? £57.50 for three of us per week.

Who arrived to see us?

The famous or infamous Dick Rowe – the boss of Decca. Famous for turning down The Beatles . . . However, he discovered not only us, but Vera Lynn, Mantovani, Tom Jones, Englebert, The Stones . . . goes on for ever! '*Oh, by the way, try 'Charmaine', Karl (Denver – a big star in the early sixties) has turned that song down, but I know it's a hit!*' How about that for a parting line from Dick?

Our first hit

What did it feel like listening to the acetate pressing of our first proper recording? Can you imagine? Did you ever get that hair on the back of your neck stand on end? Did you ever have a welling up in your eyes with sheer excitement? Did you ever just stand silent in disbelief? That numbness – it was all of that . . . and then some more.

Okay, we had a huge hit – 19 weeks in the top 20 – the longest for that year; and Con and I still sing it every time we appear on stage.

The Bachelors went to on to become one of the most successful groups of the sixties with a whole string of hits – even outselling The Beatles!

We made two films back to back (singing 'Stars Will Remember' in one and 'He's Got the Whole World in His Hands' in *He's Got a Horse* with Billy Fury – we were directed by our fantastic choreographer and lifetime friend, Ross Taylor) . . . TV series, TV appearances coming out of our ears! We played *Top of the Pops* so many times that we had our own wardrobe department at the BBC.

Where we are now

Touring, touring . . . and then more touring . . . missing our families. Con misses Kay, his childhood sweetheart and still his wife, and mother to Carole, Greg, Michael and Phillip.

On tour, I am lost without Sandy, my lifetime partner and best friend, my kids (no matter how old, they are still kids!) Victoria, Oliver and Louisa. Home with our families is our 'heaven'.

Concert tours

Of course, when Con and I do our concert tours we still have to play all the favourite 'toons', but we present them in a unique 'today' digital way . . . so you hear precisely what we all meant you to hear in the first place. Make sense?

The great honours we have had thrust upon us: headlining at Millwall Football Ground to celebrate the Queen Mum's 100th birthday. Starring in the 'Howard Keel Golf Classic' Cabaret with Johnny Mathis and Howard Keel himself! *Four* standing ovations in 20 minutes! The 'Waterfront' in Belfast, with an audience of 4,330 and six standing ovations in 30 minutes . . . unbelievable.

The fun we both have travelling around the world: it's a doddle – and we get paid for it! We get to see exciting places, meet lovely people, sing a few songs and smile at the bank manager. Who could ask for anything better?

Recording

At the time of writing, our 61st album has just been released. Did we ever think we would get this far? And the equipment available today just makes us sound better and better.

Where we will be

Our goal is to be at the very pinnacle of our skills in the year 2010.

Recording in the future?

We will use every bit of tomorrow's digital technology to enhance and improve the fantastic sounds that Con and I always make and we produce the most exciting harmonies and vocal tricks. Con's voice is a total joy to work with – such power, such genuine emotion.

The big question we get asked all the time?

'*When are you going to retire?*' Answer: I will retire five years after I die. You see, Con and I don't work; what we do is not work. What we do is what we enjoy doing and we happen to get paid for it. Think of Jack Nicklaus, the great golfer . . . does he work? Has he ever worked? Ask Richard Branson or Ross Perot, if they work. I just know the answer they will give.

As we said, Sheila and Dec are two very different singers but there are common threads to their success – perseverance at the beginning, and hard work to be able to take advantage of the 'breaks' when they showed up. Also a refusal to rest on their laurels – both singers are constantly seeking new projects and ways to use their talents in new areas. Interestingly, both Sheila and Dec prove that whether in a group or solo, it is the individual's own motivation, outlook and business-like approach that makes the difference. It is also a mark of the true star that both Sheila and Dec are actively involved in supporting and encouraging the next generation of singers. With this in mind, we would love to feature *your* successful case study in a future edition of this book. Developing the attitude that will create that success is a task you can start on right now.

With a Little Help From My Friends

A working singer's resource guide

If we tell you yet again that the best way to learn to be a working singer is to get as much practice and experience as you can, we'd be in danger of sounding like a broken record . . . but it's a refrain well worth repeating just one more time before we launch into this collection of further reading and resources to take you beyond the 'kick start' we hope you've received from this book.

There *is* lots of advice out there, and we're big believers in the credo that once you stop learning you stop living, whether you're embarking on your first ever singing lesson or your 25th world stadium tour. However, all we can do in the space we have here is list the publications, websites and organisations we've personally found interesting or helpful. Because both the industry and the content of publications and especially websites can change from year to year and edition to edition, please bear in mind that just because a resource is here doesn't mean we stand over everything contained in it – but every contact here will give you food for thought and absolutely no excuse to sit staring at your bedroom wall between gigs. And if you do come across other or better resources in your musical journey, please let us know in time for out next edition.

Publications
Singing and acting are similar professions in that, by their nature, you are not working all the time, and as someone once said the longer the gap between jobs the harder it is to convince yourself you really are a singer. Regularly reading music publications is one way to connect yourself to the industry when you're 'resting', and an essential activity if you want to keep yourself up to speed for marketing purposes. If your

budget doesn't run to buying all of these publications (and this is just the tip of the iceberg where music-related magazines are concerned!), you may be able to persuade your local library to subscribe – particularly if you can get the music librarian on side. Many of the major publications also have online editions.

We start our list with two of the most important publications.

The Stage

Stage House, 47 Bermondsey Street, London SE1 3XT
Tel: 020 7403 1818 Fax: 020 7357 9287
Website: www.the stage.co.uk
Okay, we're biased because we have both worked for it, but *The Stage* is the essential weekly newspaper of the UK entertainment industry, with a wealth of news items, articles and – most importantly – job and talent-show adverts of interest to the working singer. You can advertise your own act there, too, if you want to. You can order it from your local newsagent if they don't stock it – although many people choose to subscribe to get to those ads first!

Just as useful is *The Stage* website, which in addition to lots of new and archive material from the paper, lively discussion boards and Julie's original 'how to' article which led to the book you're reading, contains lots of useful articles on everything from getting an agent to finding work on cruise ships.

You will also find details of *Showcall*, a highly effective directory in which singers and other performers can advertise their services.

The Singer

Rhinegold Publishing, 241 Shaftesbury Avenue, London WC2H 8TF
Tel: 020 7333 1721 Fax: 020 7333 1769
Website: www.rhinegold.co.uk
The Singer provides a lively perspective on the world of song, the lives of singers and the demands of the singing profession. Covering opera, cabaret, musicals, gospel, barbershop and choral singing, the magazine brings you event and competition news, star profiles, record reviews, music reviews, health matters and plenty of tips on surviving the profession. Published bi-monthly (six issues a year).

Rhinegold Publishing also publish a wide range of respected music publications – it's well worth checking out their full catalogue.

American Songwriter
Website: www.americansongwriter.com
Although this US songwriting magazine is based in Nashville, both the publication and its associated website feature comprehensive information and resources for writers and singers from a wide range of disciplines.

BBC Music Magazine
BBC Worldwide, Woodlands, 80 Wood Lane, London
W12 0TT
Tel: 020 8576 3277 Fax: 020 8576 3292
Website: www.bbcmusicmagazine.com

Billboard
Endeavour House, 189 Shaftesbury Avenue, London WC2H 8T
Tel: 020 7420 6003 Fax: 020 7420 6014
Website: www.billboard.com
This and the two publications following are the main music industry magazines. In the first two, particularly, you'll find as much if not more about business as you will about singing – and if you have serious recording ambitions, it's the business side of the industry you need to be up to date with.

Blues and Soul
153 Praed Street, London W2 1RL
Tel: 020 7402 6869 Fax: 020 7224 8227
Email: info@bluesandsoul.co.uk
Website: www.bluesandsoul.co.uk
Very supportive of new talent in this genre.

Classical Singer
Website: www.classicalsinger.com
USA-based magazine.

Cross Rhythms

Website: www.crossrhythms.co.uk
Very respected gospel/Christian contemporary music magazine (and linked radio station) which proves that the devil not only doesn't have all the good music, he doesn't have the best music critics either.

DJ Magazine

Craven House, 121 Kingsway, London WC2B 6PA
Tel: 020 7721 8120 Fax: 020 7721 8121
Website: www.djmag.com
If you want them to play your music, you may as well try to get inside their heads!

Folk Roots (UK)

PO Box 337, London N4 1TW.
Again, a particularly supportive magazine for new talent in its area.

Guitar magazines

Too numerous to list, but there are several very good ones – you're bound to find them on the music shelf in any decent-sized newsagent. Useful for singers whether guitar players or not, as they often feature transcriptions and chords for popular and chart songs.

Kerrang!

EMAP Metro, Mappin House, 4 Winsley Street, London W1R 7AR
Tel: 020 7436 1515 Fax: 020 7312 8910
Website: www.kerrang.com
The world's top-selling rock magazine, apparently . . . but if this is your chosen style of music, you probably know that anyway. Commendably good at listing upcoming gigs by promising artists. Make sure your gig is listed (but if you're a cabaret singer don't be surprised if the crowd turns nasty!).

Music Week

Miller Freeman Entertainment, 8 Montague Close, London SE1 9UR

Tel: 020 7940 8500 Fax: 020 7407 7094
Website: www.dotmusic.co.uk

NME
New Musical Express, IPC Magazines, King's Reach Tower,
Stamford Street, London SE1 9LS
Tel: 020 7261 5813 Fax: 020 7261 5185
Website: www.nme.com

Opera Now Magazine
Website: www.opera.co.uk
Claims to be the world's most influential opera magazine.

Performing Songwriter
Website: www.performingsongwriter.com

Recording Magazine
Website: www.recordmag.com

Sing Out! The Folk Song Magazine
Website: www.singout.org
Includes complete lead sheets for traditional and contemporary
folk songs, feature articles and interviews, instrumental teach-
ins, loads of recording and book reviews, comprehensive and
up-to-date folk festival and camp listings, plus regular columns
on the folk process, songwriting, storytelling and children's
music.

Singer
Website: www.singermagazine.com
Not to be confused with *The Singer*, this US magazine also
provides lots of useful techniques, training and technology for
the vocal performer.

Smash Hits
EMAP, Mappin House, 4 Winsley House, London W1N 7AR
Tel: 020 7436 1515 Fax: 020 7636 5702
Website: www.smashhits.net
If the charts are your goal then yes, you've got to read it. And
no pretending it's for your 10-year-old niece.

MusicMagazines.com

As we, said this list is just the tip of the iceberg. If you still haven't found what you're looking for – and aren't a U2 tribute group – here's a site that you can search for any type of music magazine. It will give you contact information and a URL for the website where available. You can also try www.findarticles.com, where you can search for a wide range of music, songwriting and singing articles and critiques

Organisations

Ultimately being a singer involves being out there on stage on your own. We were about to say 'unless you're in a band', but some of our friends who've had bad band experiences might argue that being in a band can make you feel *even more* alone. Before you reach that level of cynicism, you might want to check out some of the following organisations to see what they can offer you in terms of help, advice and protection.

British Musicians Union

Website: www.musiciansunion.org.uk
The MU has a comprehensive website on which you can find out everything membership offers, along with advice on everything from music matters to health and safety.

Equity

Website: www.equity.org.uk
Although Equity is often considered to be the actors' union, members include not only singers who work in choirs, choruses and groups but also those who work as individuals in pubs, clubs and other light entertainment venues, concerts, opera, pop, theatre, recordings, sessions, radio, television, films and in places of worship.

Singers are covered in all the following Equity agreements:

• national and house agreements for opera
• West End, provincial, subsidised repertory and small-scale theatre agreements
• BBC, ITV and PACT television agreements
• BBC Radio agreement

- radio commercials agreement
- CORCA agreement for Variety artists
- BPI agreements for pop and classical recordings
- PACT cinema agreement
- classical public concerts guidelines
- TV commercials guidelines.

Equity also aims to represent members working abroad (on cruise ships, for instance) and even if a member is engaged on a non-Equity contract, is happy to give advice.

Singers' rates card
Equity produce a comprehensive guide to the minimum rates of pay for singers. This is available free of charge to any Equity member who requires it, and it is updated whenever any of these rates change.

Singers' newsletter
An overview of Equity's activities on behalf of singers is sent twice a year, free of charge to all those on the Singers' Register and to any other Equity member who requests it. Any Equity member who is a singer is entitled to go onto the Singers' Register and automatically receive the newsletter, rates card and any other information that is of specific relevance to singers.

Singers within Equity
There are two specialist committees for singers, which are made up of elected members. The Concert and Session Singers' Committee and the Opera Deputies' Committee both work hard to promote and extend the rights of the groups they represent.

There are specially reserved places for singers on the policy-making body, the Equity Council, plus places for Variety Councillors, who represent singers and others working in variety, circus and light entertainment. This level of representation within Equity means that the singers' voice is always heard when policy is being made.

There are members of staff in both the theatre/variety and film/television/radio departments who are assigned to look after singers in whatever arena of work they are engaged.

Equity's Regional Organisers are also well versed in issues affecting singers, and so help and information are never far away.

Mechanical Copyright Protection Society

Website: www.mcps.co.uk

One of the world's largest royalty collection societies, MCPS licences the recording and use of music in all its shapes and forms – from Benjamin Britten to the Beatles.

Performing Right Society

Website: www.prs.co.uk

The Performing Right Society is the UK association of composers, songwriters and music publishers. It administers the performing right in their music, in relation to the provisions of the Copyright, Designs and Patents Act 1988.

PAMRA

Website: www.pamra.co.uk

The Performing Artists Media Rights Association is the UK's collecting society for performers. For the uninitiated, that means we pay out money to qualifying performers for the broadcast of their recorded performances.

The right to receive 'royalties' for recorded performances is a relatively new one for performers in the UK. It came into law on 1 December 1996. The new law works like this: if you are a qualifying performer and have made a commercial recording since 1946, you may be due some money if your recording was broadcast or played in public since 1 December 1996 in the UK. In other words, PAMRA is not just relevant to songwriters but is also worth checking out by singers who have recorded material by other writers or are planning to.

Websites

Read our lips: if you still can't use the Internet *learn* to use the Internet – it really is the future of music, and any working singer who can't at least send and receive emails and use the net for research is unlikely to stay working much further into the century.

The Internet contains a virtual treasure trove of advice and resources no matter what your chosen area of interest. We could never list all the sites available to you – and it would be pointless also, since many sites change addresses and contents frequently. Try entering 'how to be a singer' or a similar phrase into a good search engine such as Ask Jeeves (www.ask.co.uk) or Google (www.google.com) and see what an Aladdin's cave opens out before you.

However, be aware that far more than in printed material where stricter editing and legal considerations apply, there is a huge amount of rubbish and misinformation on the Internet alongside all the invaluable information. Before you take health or legal advice, and particularly before you part with personal or credit card details, be certain to check your sources carefully.

Here are a couple of our favourite sites to start you off:

www.vocalist.org.uk
One of our very favourite sites for singers – UK-based with tons of useful information and links set out in easy-to-find style.

www.cdnow.com
One of the world's largest online record shops, with lots of downloads and artist biographies – go on, check out your competition!

Below are two more large websites with links to almost everything a professional singer, songwriter or musician could want.
www.hitsquad.com
www.singer-songwriter.com

Other useful links include:
www.musesmuse.com
A large amount of useful information, including articles on songwriting and singing, as well as a huge list of useful organisations – in particular check out the section on songwriting competitions.

www.writingsongs.com
This 'hands on' site for songwriters includes an online 'songwriter's toolbox' complete with rhyme dictionary,

thesaurus, word dictionary, guitar chord/scale finder and guitar tuner, a piano chord look-up and an appropriate Bible verse for when you need divine inspiration.

There are whole websites devoted to specific styles of music, such as:

www.jazzsingers.com

www.operastuff.com

These are just two examples – check out your own style of singing on your favourite search engine.

Message boards

In addition to information and articles, many of the big music websites have chat rooms and message boards where you can swap opinions and information with other singers. While it can be fun to interact with other people in what can often be a lonely business, remember that our advice about not getting hooked up with negativity and backbiting applies just as much on stage as it does online – some of the people you meet in cyberspace are extremely bitter and aggressive. If you intend to take part in online chat or messaging frequently it is probably best to create a separate email address for just this activity.

Books

From several hundred biographies of Elvis, from muck raking to myth making, there are far too many books on individual singers and styles of music to list here. Amazon (www.amazon.com) is one of the biggest online bookshops and as good a place as any to start looking for books that appeal to your own particular tastes.

But as a working singer we would encourage you to look further than just the music section for your inspiration. In particular we recommend that you keep an eye on bestselling business and personal development books, from Stephen Coveney's *7 Habits of Highly Effective People,* to Dale Carnegie's *The Power of Positive Thinking*. Besides helping you in other aspects of your life (and remember our maxim: get your life sorted out and your career will sort itself out), you could do yourself a lot of good by specifically thinking about how the principles contained in these books could be applied to your singing career.

We particularly recommend *Your Best Year Yet* by Jinny Ditzler (Thorsons), which is not so much a book as a three-hour life-planning workshop which will help you balance your singing goals with the rest of your activities and responsibilities. It will quite possibly be the most important three hours you spend all year.

If you would like to develop your between-song patter you could do worse than pick up John's previous book, *Writing Comedy*, which is also published by A&C Black, and if you would like to expand your singing career into other aspects of performance the companion book to this one, *An Actor's Guide to Getting Work* by Simon Dunmore, should be very useful. *Secrets of Performing Confidence* by Andrew Evans is another fascinating and practical book. Check out our own site, www.webtoonist.com for our latest books and reports which expand on themes in this book, from how to create your own one-hour show, to how to write the ultimate marketing letter.

Health services

We've already mentioned the health and safety guidelines on the Musician's Union website.

For advice on vocal health, you may find the following US websites useful – bearing in mind that there is no substitute for advice from a qualified medical practitioner:

The Voice Foundation
www.voicefoundation.org/vfvocalhealth.htm

National Center for Voice and Speech
www.ncvs.org/lifelong/strategies.html

Another site worth checking out, particularly if nerves are your problem (not to mention if smoking is messing up your vocal health!) is www.hypnotherapist-london.com – a website run by Adeline Kam, a highly qualified (and non-scary!) therapist, with a particular interest in applying hypnotherapy principles to singing and performance.

Counselling, image consultancy and training services

The Samaritans
National numbers:
In the UK dial 08457 90 90 90, for the cost of a local call.
In the Republic of Ireland dial 1850 60 90 90, for the cost of a local call.
Website: www.samaritans.co.uk
There are also local branches. Always on call 24 hours a day, completely confidential and contacted by many more singers, both unknown and world famous, than you might imagine.

Consumer Credit Counselling Service
Tel: 0800 138 1111
Website: www.cccs.co.uk
A free and confidential service that will help you get back in control of your finances.

Josh Image Consultancy
91–95 Church St, Croydon, Surrey CR0 1RN
Tel: 0208 6498919
Many image consultancies offer a 'full range of services' from hair and make-up advice to clothes and styling. The Josh organisation, based in Croydon, goes one further by offering confidential counselling by trained counsellors with a particular interest in performance and music.

Transformations
51 Crescent Road, Plaistow, London E13 0LU
Tel: 020 8470 2383
A cultural and holistic counselling service offering advice and support for dealing with life's challenges, it is particularly open to working with singers and other performers.

Christians in Entertainment
PO Box 3019, South Croydon, Surrey CR2 7PJ
Email: chris@cieweb.org.uk
As the name suggests, CIE exists to provide emotional and spiritual support to Christians working in the often lonely world

of entertainment, but it has often provided a non-threatening 'light in the darkness' for performers of little or no faith.

Crystal Business Training

17 Cavendish Square, London W1G OPH
Tel: 020 7665 1837 Fax: 020 7665 1237
Email: infocrystal@aol.com
Primarily aimed at business people, this is one of the best media training companies in the UK. Courses are personalised and therefore not cheap, but if you particularly want to target TV and corporate work, or generally improve how you put yourself across on and offstage, you couldn't be in better hands.

Taking your career to the next level ...

To finish off with, and to really help you take what we've covered in this book further, we'd like to encourage you to check out what has to be one of the most useful – and fun – websites on the net: www.make hits.com.

By now you know we're big fans of award-winning author and mega hit maker Dec Cluskey and his amazing website. (And not just us – Dec Cluskey was recently honoured as one of the top 40 most influential people of the past 40 years in the music industry by Marshall Amplification.)

Dec is a great example of the ultimate mark of a truly successful singer, the desire to put something back into the industry, and this website is the result. If this book has kick-started you on the road to success, Dec is the man to get you on the motorway.

This site really is a great resource for singers, not just because Dec's courses and regular emailings are chock-a-block with solid advice and encouragement, but also because his forthright and provocative writing style are a breath of fresh air in an industry where flattery and false promises are the order of the day.

Dec answers all emails personally-and has set up a special email address (John-Julie@makehits.com) where readers of this book will get an especially warm welcome. In the meantime, our warmest thanks for reading this far. Happy reading, surfing and singing!

John and Julie
April 2003

Index